E=M

Making Poems for America
ROBERT FROST

Britannica Bookshelf—Great Lives Series

Making Poems for America

ROBERT FROST

by Gorham Munson

Illustrated by Dan Siculan

B
F92m

Published by
ENCYCLOPAEDIA BRITANNICA PRESS, INC., Chicago

PM JH

Poem and parts of poems and other matter from *Complete Poems of Robert Frost* (1949) and *In the Clearing* (1962) are reprinted by the permission of the publishers, Holt, Rinehart & Winston, Inc.

Other quotations are used by permission of the publishers from Reginald L. Cook, *The Dimensions of Robert Frost* (Rinehart, 1958); Elizabeth Shepley Sergeant, *Robert Frost: The Trial by Existence* (Holt, 1960); Richard Thornton, *Recognition of Robert Frost* (Holt, 1937); Cornelius Weygandt, *The White Hills* (Holt, 1934); Lawrance Thompson, *Fire and Ice* (Holt, 1942); Sidney Cox, *A Swinger of Birches* (New York University Press, 1957); Ezra Pound, *Letters* (Harcourt, 1950); Charles Norman, *Ezra Pound* (Macmillan, 1960); Rinna Sammel, "Robert Frost in Israel," *New York Times Book Review,* April 23, 1961; Robert Frost, "Between Prose and Verse," *Atlantic Monthly,* January, 1962; *Book of the Month Club News,* May, 1936; Mark Van Doren, "The Permanence of Robert Frost," *The American Scholar,* Winter, 1936; Robert Frost, "Perfect Day—a Day of Prowess," *Sports Illustrated,* July 23, 1956; reviews of *A Boy's Will* and *North of Boston* in *Poetry, Times Literary Supplement, Daily News* (now *News Chronicle*) and *The New Republic.*

TABLE OF CONTENTS

Chapter 1

"A Day of Days"

About noon on Thursday, January 19, 1961, snow began to fall on Washington, D.C. It was a stinging, blinding snowfall that brought concern to the thousands who had filled the hotels, boardinghouses, and motels of the nation's capital. What effect, they wondered, would this ominous weather have on tomorrow's spectacle—the Inauguration of John Fitzgerald Kennedy?

The anxiety turned to confusion as six inches of snow—unusual for Washington—piled up. Thousands of automobiles were stalled and abandoned. Stacked-up airplanes had to turn back over the snow-swept airport.

Among the many who found it hard that night to get through the snow-choked streets was a man who is justly called America's Grand Old Man of Poetry, Robert Frost. On this Inaugural Eve he was still hale in this 86th year. True, he now walked slowly, he who had been a great walker most of his life—"I have outwalked the furthest city light," he had written—but his big countryman's frame was still strong. And he was still young in spirit. He always looked to the future the way youth does, and this night he was as excited about the next four years as the young men who had come to Washington to assume national office.

Through the long, snowy evening Robert Frost was buoyant and gay in the home of the new Secretary of the Interior, Stewart Lee Udall. He was stimulated by the thought that the next day was to be, in his own words, "for my cause a day of days." Two years earlier, when he had been Consultant in Poetry to the Library of Congress, Frost had complained to reporters that no one in Congress consulted him. Udall, then a Congressman from Arizona, had decided to change that situation. He invited Frost to his home to meet a number of Congressmen. From this meeting, a friendship grew between Frost and Udall. Then Udall had had an inspiration: he suggested to President-elect Kennedy that he invite Frost to take part in the Inauguration.

Inauguration Day—Friday, January 20th—was cold and clear, and a glare of sunshine reflected from the snow. The poet mingled with the great figures of the nation—Justices of the Supreme Court, United States Senators and Representatives, Cabinet officers, the Joint Chiefs of Staff, the outgoing President and the family of the incoming President—on the inaugural platform on Capitol Plaza. He cast a friendly look at the great mass of spectators in front of the stands and smiled at the ingenious ways some of them had dressed for warmth against the cold, stiff wind.

The Marine Band struck up "America the Beautiful." Marian Anderson sang "The Star-Spangled Banner." And then came a lengthy invocation spoken by Richard Cardinal Cushing of Boston. The oath of Vice President was taken by Lyndon Baines Johnson. Now came Frost's part in the program, and the

"This day is—for my cause—a day of days."

poet stepped to the lectern, holding a manuscript.

He had received many honors in his long lifetime. Four times he had been given the Pulitzer Prize. He had been showered with honorary degrees from American universities. Oxford and Cambridge in England had conferred degrees on him. On his 75th birthday the United States Senate had passed a resolution to honor him. Only a year before, Congress had awarded him a medal. But the invitation to read a poem at the Inauguration was the greatest honor of all. In his long career this was the highest peak of recognition.

The glint of sun off the snow almost spoiled it. As he stood at the lectern, the brilliant light blinded him.

Frost's voice faltered. A wave of sympathy rose toward him as he struggled to read the verse preface to his famous poem, "The Gift Outright." But fear struck the radio audience that could only hear the hesitantly read, halting lines:

> *Summoning artists—to participate*
> *In the August—occasions—of the state*
> *Seems something—for us—all—to celebrate.*
> *This day is—for my cause—a day of days.*

The voice stopped.

A fearful question leaped to the minds of millions of radio listeners: Has the poet collapsed? But those who could see—the television viewers and the spectators on Capitol Plaza—knew that the poet was all right. They could guess that the glare made the words unseeable. They saw Vice President Johnson try to help the poet by shielding the paper with his top hat. But Frost had to give up the attempt to read the 42-line preface.

Then, just as the radio listeners felt sharply apprehensive,

Frost raised his head and in strong, vibrant, passionate tones he said from memory the great lines of "The Gift Outright."

> The land was ours before we were the land's.
> She was our land more than a hundred years
> Before we were her people. She was ours
> In Massachusetts, in Virginia,
> But we were England's, still colonials,
> Possessing what we still were unpossessed by,
> Possessed by what we now no more possessed.
> Something we were withholding made us weak
> Until we found out that it was ourselves
> We were withholding from our land of living,
> And forthwith found salvation in surrender.
> Such as we were we gave ourselves outright
> (The deed of gift was many deeds of war)
> To the land vaguely realizing westward,
> But still unstoried, artless, unenhanced,
> Such as she was, such as she would become.

What more appropriate poem than this one about the meaning of the American Revolution could have been selected for the Inauguration? Although written as long ago as 1935, it had not been publicly read until December 5, 1941—two days before disaster at Pearl Harbor. Printed soon afterward, it was widely read by men in the armed forces, among them Lieutenant John Fitzgerald Kennedy of the PT 109. It had grown famous through the stresses of the Cold War years when Americans looked for a fresh pledge of giving themselves outright to their native land.

For the Inauguration, Kennedy had asked Frost to alter

the last line to read: "Such as she was, such as she will become."
But the poet could not bring himself to make the change from
"would" to "will". He recited the original line and then added
the revised line with a notice that the change was for this special
occasion only. Thus he kept the integrity of "The Gift Outright."
A few minutes later President Kennedy was redefining "the gift
outright" in his Inaugural Address.

Poet and President thought and felt alike on the meaning
of America. There was a real bond between the youthful President, aged 43, and the venerable poet, aged 86. The next day
Frost was the first official visitor to the White House and was
taken on a tour of the mansion by the President himself. A few
weeks later, in a television program, the President hailed the
bond of admiration and affection between him and Frost. "I
asked Robert Frost," he said, "to come and speak at the Inauguration not merely because I was desirous of according a
recognition to his trade, but also because I felt that he had
something important to say to those of us who were occupied
with the business of government; that he would remind us that
we were dealing with life, the hopes and fears of millions of
people, and also tell us that our own deep convictions must be
the ultimate guide of all our actions."

He also said: "I've never taken the view that the world of
politics and the world of poetry are so far apart. I think politi-
cians and poets share at least one thing, and that is that their
greatness depends upon the courage with which they face the
challenge of life."

In comment on the new President's faith, Frost said:
"We've decided to go the length, decided to go the length and
lead from our strength. We're going to go the length and lead

from our strength, not from our timidity and weakness, but lead like fighting, you know, from our strength. Sum it all up in saying, an Augustan age of poetry and power, with the emphasis on the power. That belongs to my poetry, and it belongs to politics all the time."

Chapter 2

"Such Was Life in the Golden Gate"

R obert Lee Frost was born in San Francisco on March 26, 1874. A boy's life there had a flavor that could even be tasted, as Frost later made clear in a poem:

> *A Peck of Gold*
> *Dust always blowing about the town,*
> *Except when sea-fog laid it down,*
> *And I was one of the children told*
> *Some of the blowing dust was gold.*
>
> *All the dust the wind blew high*
> *Appeared like gold in the sunset sky,*
> *But I was one of the children told*
> *Some of the dust was really gold.*
>
> *Such was life in the Golden Gate:*
> *Gold dusted all we drank and ate,*
> *And I was one of the children told,*
> *'We all must eat our pack of gold.'*

The poet's father, William Prescott Frost, Jr., was a restless New Englander who had caught the spirit of the Far West. A brilliant student at Harvard, he had graduated *cum laude* with a Phi Beta Kappa key in 1872, but he had been unsettled by the Civil War. Though a New Englander, he had sympathized with the South and had even thought of running away to join the Confederate army, but he had been too young. Southern sympathizers like him in the North were called Copperheads, and in San Francisco in 1874, William Prescott Frost, Jr., was still a Copperhead. He showed it when his son was born by christening him Robert Lee Frost, naming him for the great Confederate general. Robert's father, a vigorous extremist States' Rights man, once pointed to a map of the United States and said to his son as he carved out five sections with his finger, "Here, these are the five nations into which our country will split."

An energetic and risk-taking man was William Prescott Frost, Jr. He needed to be, for he was a newspaperman in the days when the windows of the *Bulletin,* the paper he worked for, were shot out by men angry at its stock market news. Men in San Francisco frequently wore revolvers as an article of dress. Robert Frost remembers a Sunday afternoon walk he and some other children took with his father and a few of his father's friends. They found a bottle, stoppered it, and tossed it into the Bay. Out came revolvers of all the men, and a flurry of shots sank the improvised target.

Robert's father was a politician too, a Democrat, the friend of Chris Buckley, the notoriously corrupt, blind boss of San Francisco. But the elder Frost was also the friend of the incorruptible Henry George, the author of *Progress and Poverty,* who had once worked in the composing room of the

Bulletin. The reformer sought in his book to explain the hard times that had come upon the country and to solve them by advocating reform in the taxation of land. At first, few people read *Progress and Poverty,* but by the time Robert Frost was in high school, it became an international best seller. In later years, he liked to recall that he had known George when he was little known.

As for Robert's schooling, he was envied by other boys because his father often kept him out of school to run political errands. When his father was a candidate for tax collector of San Francisco, his ten-year-old son tagged along to the saloons where his father did his electioneering. The boy had to become a good marksman of an odd sort. His job was to fling the campaign cards of W. P. Frost, Jr., to the ceiling. Each card had a tack through it, and the trick was to use a silver dollar as a kind of flying mallet to hammer the card to the ceiling. Robert became quite skilled at this trick. But the Republicans defeated W. P. Frost, Jr.

Every Fourth of July, Robert's father broke loose. The elder Frost liked to speculate wildly in the stock market, and he celebrated Independence Day in the same wild spirit. It was neither safe nor sane the way he celebrated it. He made the most noise possible, set fire to outhouses, and did other minor property damage. He went the limit, too, in political celebrations and took Robert with him. The boy rode in costume on floats in big parades or trudged in torchlight processions until he was sent home worn out.

When he was five or six years old, Rob Frost had an experience that planted unforgettable impressions. The small boy watched a mighty storm from the Cliff House, a San Fran-

[*17*]

cisco resort with a platform enabling one to look far out to sea. Here he felt something that only years later could he put into words in the poem "Once by the Pacific."

> *The shattered water made a misty din.*
> *Great waves looked over others coming in,*
> *And thought of doing something to the shore*
> *That water never did to land before.*
> *The clouds were low and hairy in the skies,*
> *Like locks blown forward in the gleam of eyes.*

The might of this storm made a wordless impression of a great doom to be endured by the planet, an impression remembered in maturity:

> *There would be more than ocean-water broken*
> *Before God's last* Put out the Light *was spoken.*

Rob's boyhood knowledge of his father undoubtedly had something to do with his early sense of a tragic meaning in life. The boy sadly saw his father's health decline as tuberculosis gained the upper hand. His father was as reckless about his health as he was about the stock market, politics, and the Fourth of July. He would swim far out into Sausalito Bay with Rob watching him from the beach, but his strength would give out and he would be scarcely able to reach shore again. Then he would drag himself to his "medicine bottle" full of whiskey. His father would tell the family he would make some lucky strike and then he would take a trip to "the Islands"—to Hawaii, a favored resort for tuberculosis patients. But the lucky strike never came. Meanwhile he drank to allow him to keep up his hectic pace, and he drank warm blood at the stockyards—a

[*18*]

horrid remedy—to combat the ravages of tuberculosis, and whooped it up in politics. At the age of 34, William Prescott, Jr., was burned out. Rob Frost was 11 years old when his father died in his own house in the arms of a political crony.

One day early in May of 1885 Rob, his little sister Jeanie, and his mother Belle Frost began the long railroad journey back to New England. In the baggage car rode the coffined body of the handsome, restless father to its last resting-place. The mother and the two children sorrowed for the lost father and could not help wishing miserably that he had paid the last premiums on his life insurance. But he had neglected to do so, and the expectation of $20,000 insurance money vanished. They would have to seek aid from the parents of their improvident father.

A bereft boy stared out the coach window on his sad way East.

Rob didn't know then what to think of his father. He remembered an awful occasion when his father had given him a

[*19*]

quarter and sent him out to buy cigarettes. As he was running to the store, the quarter slipped from his hand and fell into a crack of the board sidewalk. In vain he tried to recover the quarter, and passersby were unable to find it. The quarter was gone. Frantic, Rob went to the store, fearfully explained that he had dropped his money, and begged for a package of cigarettes. The clerk and the men standing about only laughed. There was nothing to do but return home in fear and tell his mother. Father was waiting in his study and by now was no doubt impatient for a smoke. His mother also stood in fear of Father's anger, but in this case she decided that Rob was the one to go in and tell of the loss. Only first let them pray, mother and son, that Rob would be let off unpunished. Then Rob went in and reported the disaster. Well, there was no telling how his father would take things. This time he merely glanced up from something he was writing, said brusquely "Never mind," and turned back to complete his sentence.

Robert kept back his tears as the train headed east.

At 41, Isabelle Moodie Frost knew that she had to take up school teaching again. She had taught mathematics for seven years at Columbus, Ohio, and then had joined the staff at Bucknell Academy in Pennsylvania. It was there that a temporary teacher, William Prescott, Jr., had wooed her with an old quatrain that perfectly suited his character. Robert Frost remembers that his father loved to declaim:

He either fears his fate too much,
  Or his deserts are small,
That dares not put it to the touch,
  To gain or lose it all.

[20]

Well, he had lost it all, this "double or nothing" man, and from now on it would be Frost's Scottish mother who would exercise the greater influence on her children, especially on Rob.

William Prescott Frost, Jr., and Isabelle Moodie had been a good-looking couple, and they had passed their good looks on to their son Rob. She has been described as having a pure young profile, with a long nose; full, firm, well-cut lips; and sparkling, humorous blue eyes. The description could do for Robert's countenance too.

Rob seems to have acquired most of his early literary taste from his mother, who loved romantic poetry and liked to recite Poe's "The Raven" and "Annabel Lee." Rob differed from many boys who grow up to be writers. He was not a voracious reader. Not until he was 14 did he begin to enjoy reading to himself. He was an author before he was a reader, for he began in San Francisco a serial story that he told to himself. It was about the doings of a lost and forgotten tribe that lived in a ravine no one in the outside world knew. Perhaps he put himself to sleep on that unhappy train ride East by dreaming of this inaccessible and sometimes happy tribe defending its canyon. After he came East, he continued this serial from time to time, filling in details of scenery and inhabitants, and found that it was tranquilizing to dream about it when he went to sleep.

At last the tiresome trip ended in the smoky factory town, Lawrence, Massachusetts. William Prescott Frost, Sr., was there to greet them. He seemed quite old to Rob—men in their 60's were then considered old. Grandfather seemed quite the oppo-

[21]

site of the father they had come to bury in the Lawrence grave-yard. It was hard to believe that Grandfather Frost had once aspired to be a well-dressed young blood, but that had been long ago. The New England cult of thrift and respectability had claimed him, and he had become a saver of pieces of his income and a local pillar of respectability. He had wrested a livelihood from his job as overseer in a Lawrence textile mill, and had even piled up savings. The time was to come when those savings would be most helpful to Rob during his adventure in England, but that was years ahead. To young Rob, his grandfather was a man of severity and power.

Yet there was a liberal streak in the senior William Prescott Frost. He tolerated the notions and conduct of his wife, who was one of the earliest feminists in America. Grandmother Frost had a stateliness that was enhanced by a habit of nodding her head as if in dignified resentment at the ascendancy of the male in old-time New England. One day she decided that housework was not exclusively the business of women. Summoning her husband to a conference, she called for a division of the household tasks, and right then her husband showed his liberal streak. He gave in to her demands to share the sweeping and dishwashing; and from then on, turn and turn about, one performed the services of the house while the other enjoyed a life of leisure.

Belle and her two children stayed only briefly with Grandmother and Grandfather Frost. The fatherless family soon went to live with Great Aunt Sarah Frost Messer at Amherst, New Hampshire.

Chapter 3

Valedictorian

"That Rob can do anything," his mother used to say. It is quite probable that she said this to herself when she attended the graduation exercises of the class of 1892 of Lawrence High School. She had reason to be especially proud of Robert on that occasion, for her son was the star performer. The program said that the class hymn set to Beethoven's music had been composed by Robert Lee Frost, and the valedictory was to be given by the same student.

Mother and son had indeed hoed a hard row together to reach this evening of triumph. She had herself prepared Rob to enter Lawrence High School in the fall of 1888. They had lived around with relatives for almost a year after coming East. Rob and his sister Jeanie had at first been scornful of this East for which their father had expressed no love. They encountered pennies for the first time, and they made up a game to express their scorn of people who used "chicken feed" for currency. First, they would hold up a nickel and say, "San Francisco!" Then they would pinch a penny and say, "Boston!" But this childish snobbishness had not lasted long. Quite soon they were little New Englanders.

[23]

As she had foreseen on the train ride, Isabelle Frost had had to resume teaching, and in the spring of 1886 she took a district school in Salem, New Hampshire. She moved there with her two children and enrolled them in the district school. She seems to have been a very good teacher with some original methods. For instance, she seated her 34 pupils according to the ability they showed, and she gave them individual instruction. They liked to hear her read aloud. But the salary was only $9 a week for a school year of 36 weeks, which added up to only $324 a year. And so it was necessary for Rob to get odd jobs. He worked in a shoe shop when he was 12, inserting nails in the heels of shoes.

When he was 14, Rob entered the wonderful world of books on his own. He had enjoyed being read to by his mother. His favorite book had been *Tom Brown's School Days;* but he had never let her finish, for he could not bear the thought that he had heard the whole tale. Nor did he finish the first book he read himself, Jane Porter's *The Scottish Chiefs,* which was then very popular with young readers. Rob said that he didn't read through the last chapter because he already "knew the end."

Miss Susan Nash and Robert became partners in getting out a newspaper. Susan had a tiny printing press and Rob had the initiative. He was the editor and printer. The news came from other papers and magazines, items that Rob and Susan thought might interest their readers—friends and neighbors to whom Susan sold the paper.

Behind the selection of Robert Lee Frost as class poet lay the first stirrings of Robert Frost the poet. His Scottish mother had read to him the poems of Robert Burns and Sir Walter Scott. He had read with eagerness the poems of William Cullen

Bryant and Edgar Allan Poe. He went on to Shelley's "Alastor" and Keats's "Endymion," but found them too much for him. A new book, the story of a wealthy Bostonian who was hypnotized and awoke in 2000 A.D. to find himself in a utopian society, had also come his way. This was the quickly famous *Looking Backward,* published in 1888, by Edward Bellamy. It wasn't poetry, but it engaged young Frost's social imagination. But the one book that triggered the poetic impulse of Robert Frost was *The History of the Conquest of Mexico* by William Hickling Prescott. In his history class Rob was required to read about Cortez in Prescott's book. It appealed to Rob because Prescott wrote excitingly and glamorously about the civilization of Montezuma and the Spanish conquistadors who conquered Mexico in the 16th century. Rob was thrilled by Prescott's narrative power and found himself deeply sympathetic with the Indians who resisted Cortez. Rob was descended from Indian fighters in the colonies; but one of his passions in boyhood was angry sympathy with the people who fought his ancestors, and this sympathy stretched back to the Aztecs under Montezuma.

Quite unexpectedly when school let out after this history lesson, Rob found himself dwelling on an incident that befell a group of Aztecs who might "just have turned the tide" on that *noche triste,* that terrible night, when the Spaniards fought their way out of the capital city of the Aztecs. As Rob walked home from school, he recalls that "there was a wind and darkness. I had never written a poem before, and as I walked, it appeared like a revelation, and I became so taken by it that I was late at my grandmother's." Arriving there, he immediately sat down to the kitchen table and wrote out the poem, a narra-

[25]

tive in ballad form, just as he had conceived it on the road. "La Noche Triste" he titled it.

The next day he took "La Noche Triste" to Ernest C. Jewell, who was two classes ahead of him and was editor of *The Bulletin,* the Lawrence High School magazine. Jewell was the first editor to accept work from Frost. Years later he sent Jewell a copy of his first book with a letter, saying, "You always believed in me as a—what shall I say?—as an intelligence and as an honest man, I think, at least in intention. And perhaps you believed in me as a poet. I never was quite sure of that. But really I am going to be justified of my poetry before the end." Young Jewell also took a fragment from Robert entitled "Tenochtitlan" (Montezuma's capital) and published both in the April, 1890 number of *The Bulletin.*

Rob followed this first breakthrough into print with another poem in the May, 1890 *Bulletin,* "The Song of the Wave." A whole year passed before Rob's next work, "A Dream of Julius Caesar," appeared in *The Bulletin* of May, 1891. In the December, 1891 issue the young poet turned to prose with an essay on the ancient site of Petra, the rock city of Jordan.

In his senior year, Rob Frost was elected editor of *The Bulletin* and experienced the nightmare of all editors, a dearth of contributors. Contributions were promised but did not come in before the deadline. Rob thereupon wrote the contents of one entire issue, using pen names freely, and then immediately resigned his editorship.

The honors Rob won at Lawrence High School were not all of a literary or academic kind. He had been popular throughout the four years. He played end on the football team but somehow escaped playing on the baseball team. Even before he had left San Francisco, he had become a baseball fan and remained one all his life. At first he had rooted for Cap Anson and the Chicago team in the old National League. Later, like all good New Englanders, he picked the Boston Red Sox in the Ameri-

"The poet's insight is his after-thought."

can League as "his" team. "I pitched a little as a boy," Frost has said. "Among the other worries about me in Lawrence was that I was getting ambitious about baseball."

He had been a poor boy throughout his high school course. At the beginning he had lived at Salem and commuted on the train. Grandfather Frost had furnished the railroad fare and Grandmother Frost the clothes—a cut-down suit of Grandfather's. Soon after Rob started, Great Uncle Elihu Colcord had given Rob his first "boughten" suit. Rob took to Greek and Latin, standard courses in those days, and kept a lifelong interest in them. At spelling he was not so good.

And now here he was at the graduation exercises. He had picked an extraordinary title for his valedictory address: "A Monument to After-Thought Unveiled." Some of the sentences his classmates heard were extraordinary, too. "The afterthought of one action," said the young orator, "is the forethought of the next." And "the poet's insight is his afterthought. It is of varied heartbeats and converse with nature. And the grandest of his ideas come when the last line is written." At the age of 18, Rob had found his own way with words.

Oddly enough, there was a second valedictory essay listed on the program: "Conversation as a Force in Life." And there was a second valedictorian: Elinor Miriam White.

This was most unusual—two valedictorians for the class of 1892. Rob Frost had led his class for the first three years; but in the fourth year a girl, doing the whole high school course in two and a half years, had caught up with him.

The head of the school had said to Rob, "Do you realize that Miss White is catching up—she may get the valedictory?"

"Give it to her now," Rob had replied.

[28]

The school head wouldn't, Frost remembers, but instead declared a tie in scholarship.

Rob's generous feeling toward his rival is easily explained. Already he was strongly drawn to her and wished her to triumph. Elinor White's father was a Universalist minister who had become a woodworker. Her ancestry went back to Peregrine White, who was born on the *Mayflower* as she lay at anchor in Cape Cod bay, the first child born of English parents in New England.

Elinor was as bright as Rob, and the decision of the school head to call their scholarship race a dead heat was wise. Perhaps he even foresaw that the two valedictorians would fall in love with each other.

Chapter 4

"I Gnaw Wood"

Life opened before Rob Frost as he left Lawrence High School at the age of 18. But what road should he take? He was undecided. Twenty-two years later he was to write in one of his best known poems, "The Road Not Taken,"

> *Two roads diverged in a yellow wood,*
> *And* [I was] *sorry I could not travel both*
> *And be one traveler . . .*

In high school Rob Frost had been a "regular fellow" and his family now expected him to do the "regular thing"—to attend college, and after that achieve a conventional success in the world, in business or in one of the professions. But the seed of nonconformity had sprouted in the young man. He didn't know if he wanted to go to college or not.

Grandmother decided for him, and Grandfather put up the money for his freshman year. His high school mathematics teacher recommended Dartmouth at Hanover, New Hampshire, and to Dartmouth Rob went in the fall of 1892. Perhaps Elinor White's decision to go to college—she chose St. Lawrence University in upstate New York—had something to do with

Rob's agreeing to go to college. As an added inducement, the offer of a fellowship reduced his tuition to $10 a year.

Rob Frost did not arrive at Hanover bursting with "college spirit." He was quickly pledged to a very good fraternity, Theta Delta Chi, and a rich classmate paid his initiation fee—evidence that he could have become popular. But he did not seem to enjoy his courses—he took 16 hours of classes a week, ran every day to compulsory chapel prayers, and heard a Sunday sermon besides—nor did he enjoy any of the extracurricular activities except "the savage rushes of those wild days," as roughhousing was called. He made only one friend, Preston Shirley, who, Frost recalls, "never missed a chance to take part with his fists" in these "rushes." "Our high old talks," Frost remembers, "about religion, politics, and history were almost as turbulent." But although Rob joined in the roughhousing, he was not, he says, a good fraternity brother and became unsocial. He liked to take long, solitary walks in the woods, night or day—all his life he was to love walking—and this unconventional activity, this walking *alone,* aroused the curiosity of his fraternity brothers. What did he do all alone in the woods? they demanded.

"I gnaw wood," was Rob's laconic reply.

On these walks came intimations of Rob's vocation of poetry. Religious people in Frost's youth spoke of "a calling" to the ministry, and poetry to him was to be a sort of "calling." Lines of poetry came to him on his walks, and he wrote them down afterwards. A few lines of "Once by the Pacific," completed much later, were first written at Dartmouth.

One afternoon in the Dartmouth library he saw a copy of a magazine called *The Independent*. This discovery turned out to be far more important for him than any he made in a class-room. He had not known that there was in America a publication publishing and featuring poetry. On the front page of this number of *The Independent* was a poem, "Seaward," by Richard Hovey, a Dartmouth graduate. "There was even an editorial about this poem," Frost has said, "which I read with rapt amaze." This experience was a revelation. There was a place in America for poetry such as Rob aspired to write. And so, when later he had a poem ready to send out, he sent it to *The Independent,* and from that came a friendship with the editors.

But Rob had had enough of college. He gave himself the excuse that his mother needed him to take care of some unruly boys in her school, but he did not fool himself. "I had decided that I was up to no good at Dartmouth, so I just went home to Methuen." He sat up all night with Preston Shirley, "carrying on and saying good-bye," and then he left without giving notice to the dean or saying good-bye to anyone else.

Only a lucky few went to college in those days, and he had been a lucky one. But he had not stayed even long enough to take his term examinations. And now he was back in Lawrence, caning "bad" boys at his mother's little school and taking a small job in a textile mill that anybody could fill. He wasn't at all like that girl, Elinor White, who had tied him for valedictorian and in whom he had been interested. She was getting excellent marks at her college. Rob seemed to be just a drifter.

In the summer of 1893 Rob's grandmother died, still puzzled by her grandson's indecision. Elinor came home for vacation, bright and beautiful, and Rob spent a good deal of time with her. In the fall she returned to St. Lawrence to resume the speeded-up pace of her studies; for Elinor, who had finished high school in record time, was aiming to complete the four-year college course in three years.

In contrast, Robert got an unskilled job in the dynamo room of the Arlington mill. His duties were simple. He had to keep an eye on the arc lights and replace the carbon when it was consumed. On bright days the arc lights were not used; and on such days Rob would climb to a secluded spot under the great belts and read a small volume of Shakespeare. On the night shift he was sometimes joined by a fellow worker, Ed Gilbert, and the two young unskilled workers read the plays together.

Rob and Ed read Shakespeare when work was slack in the mill.

Rob was getting a taste of factory life. He came to be known as a poet "versed in country things," but he was not unversed in factory things; his firsthand knowledge of the harsh side of industrial life has helped to keep his views of life in balance. Rob Frost knew well the ringing of the mill bell to warn the tardy to reach the entrance before the gate shut them out, he knew the shaking of the straining mill as its heavy machinery operated, he knew the inside scene. Later he was to describe it.

The air was full of dust of wool.
A thousand yarns were under pull. . . .

Outside the mill a cloud of poetry filled the mind of Rob, and occasionally he tried to write a poem of his own. One day in the fall of 1893, he found the wing of a dead butterfly. The flowers of summer were dead, too, and all the butterflies were gone. Rob studied the splendor of that wing, began to think of the wild flights it had made, felt tenderness for its fragility —and found himself caught up in wonder and a strange sorrow. He walked home to his frame house, locked himself in the kitchen to keep out his inquisitive sister Jeanie, and "all in one go," as he later described it, wrote the poem "My Butterfly."

This was his first poem published in a magazine for adult readers, and the first poem he was paid for. It is the earliest poem included in his first book, *A Boy's Will.* He retained it in the *Complete Poems of Robert Frost,* published 36 years later.

Why has Robert Frost continued to include "My Butterfly" in *Complete Poems?* It has artificial diction that he long ago abandoned. He has dropped "thine" and "thee," "oft" and "I wist" for the colloquial vocabulary of New England. He has passed beyond the romantic influence of Shelley and Keats, discernible in this youthful poem. In spite of all this, he has saved "My Butterfly" because the second stanza is, as he has put it, "the beginning of *me.*" Here it is:

The gray grass is scarce dappled with the snow;
Its two banks have not shut upon the river;
But it is long ago—
It seems forever—
Since first I saw thee glance,
With all thy dazzling other ones,
In airy dalliance,
Precipitate in love,
Tossed, tangled, whirled and whirled above,
Like a limp rose-wreath in a fairy dance.

" 'Its two banks have not shut upon the river'—I got something there," he said late in life, "and I knew it. But especially the last figure: *'Like a limp rose-wreath in a fairy dance.'* That's like a blush."

Full of excitement and hope, Rob sent "My Butterfly" to *The Independent.* Back came a note of acceptance from the editor, Dr. William Hayes Ward. Rob was overjoyed, as any young writer is, by his first acceptance, and replied: "The memory of your note will be a fresh pleasure to me when I waken for a good many mornings to come."

Dr. Ward wished to be helpful. He sent his young contributor a copy of a new edition of Sidney Lanier's *Poems,* which included a "Memorial" Dr. Ward had written; and he suggested that Frost study Lanier's book, *The Science of English Verse.* He suggested also that Frost return to Dartmouth. Rob would have none of Dr. Ward's advice to study Lanier's theory that the physical laws of music and poetry were the same. That might be all very well for Lanier who was a professional flutist, but Frost knew instinctively that musical versification would not be his way. Young Frost had something different in mind although he could not yet put into words his future creed of the "talk-song."

Frost gratefully wrote letters to *The Independent,* and Dr. Ward's sister and assistant, Miss Susan Hayes Ward, answered them. He told her a lot about himself. "I read novels," he said, "in the hope of strengthening my executive faculties. . . . Thomas Hardy has taught me the good use of a few words and . . . Scott and Stevenson inspire me, by their prose, with the thought that we Scotchmen are bound to be romanticists—poets. Then as for poems my favorites are and have been these: Keats' 'Hyperion,' Shelley's 'Prometheus,' Tennyson's 'Morte D'Arthur,' and Browning's 'Saul'—all of them about the giants."

In a letter to Miss Ward on August 22, 1894 from Boston, he wrote: "It is only a matter of time now when I shall throw off the mask and declare for literature mean it poverty or riches." Robert L. Frost, as he signed this letter, was turning to the road he would eventually take.

The course of his friendship with Elinor White was becoming difficult. He had not seen much of her during her second year at St. Lawrence. Then in the summer of 1894 she had taken a job with a composer in Boston. Finally she came back to Lawrence, and Rob called on her. But the president of St. Lawrence was visiting at her home, and she did not invite Rob to come in. "I must have looked awful to Elinor," the poet has reminisced. He was persuaded that Elinor didn't love him. He quit. Later a letter came from her, calling him back.

Rob decided that he would show her that he was not the ne'er-do-well some people accused him of being. He would

[*37*]

give her a book of his poems. It was a bold plan. He had five poems for his book: "My Butterfly" accepted by *The Independent* but not yet published, and four others which he has not cared to preserve in *Complete Poems*. He went to a job printer in Lawrence, selected pebbled leather for the binding and fine linen paper for the text, and gave a print order for two copies. This was to be a most limited edition indeed. One copy was to go to Elinor, one was to be kept by the poet, and then the type was to be distributed.

Off went the young poet to Canton, New York, to give Elinor her copy of *Twilight* and to press his suit for her hand. But Elinor was in an offish mood and under the influence of professors who were unimpressed by a mill hand-poet. Rob felt rebuffed and betrayed. How badly he was hurt is shown by the fact that he tore up his precious copy of *Twilight* and ran away down South.

Not much is known about the weeks of despair that followed. Robert Frost has always been closemouthed about his private life, and for long he referred to this dark period only as a brief tramping tour down South. Nobody at the time knew where he went. He gave no address to anybody, sent no news home. Not until his poem, "Kitty Hawk," was published in 1957 did his friends learn that he had wandered about North Carolina. At last he told:

> *. . . When I came here young*
> *Out and down along*
> *Past Elizabeth City*
> *Sixty years ago.*
> *I was to be sure*

[*38*]

Out of sorts with Fate,
Wandering to and fro
In the earth alone,
You might think too poor-
Spirited to care
Who I was or where
I was being blown
Faster than my tread—
Like a crumpled, better
Left-unwritten letter
I had read and thrown.

By December Rob was back in Lawrence, silent about his wandering, but greatly encouraged to find at home the issue of *The Independent* for November 8, 1894, with "My Butterfly" conspicuous on the front page. At last! He sat down to write his thanks to Miss Ward. He explained (to her but not to his friends in later life) that "four weeks ago and until Friday last I was in Virginia, North Carolina, and Maryland, very literally and without address, so that I have not been aware of my own doings as expressed in the phrase I 'published a poem.' . . . I thank you tardily because I for my part have been out of time a little while . . . And the poem does look well— don't you think it does?"

Elinor came home for Christmas vacation. There was an emotional storm from which she and Rob emerged engaged to be married. She went back to St. Lawrence to complete her course and Rob, the part-time school teacher in his mother's school and mill hand of sorts, got a new job: reporter for the weekly *Lawrence Sentinel.*

Chapter 5

"Give Me Twenty"

T he reporting job on the Sentinel didn't last long. He quit in March of 1895. He didn't like reporting at all. It seemed to him to be an energetic inquiring—"prying" was what he called it—into other people's affairs. Reticent himself, he wanted to respect the private lives of others. So his father's profession was not for him.

The *Sentinel,* however, offered Frost a chance to get in print the kind of writing this misfit reporter liked to do. Rob started a little miscellany department—a column it would be called today—and in it he put little sketches of Lawrence life: a ragged child picking coal in the railroad yard; a stray eagle that lit on the flagpole of the post office and was shot—to Robert's indignation.

Rob job-hopped from reporting back to teaching, this time at a district school in Salem, Massachusetts. He lightened his teaching days by sending love letters to Elinor at St. Lawrence. In the summer he tutored some boys. Elinor came home after graduation at St. Lawrence.

Rob's mother continued to make new plans for earning a living. Why not start a school that would enlist all her immediate family, including her prospective daughter-in-law? So she opened a private school with about 20 pupils at Lawrence in the fall of 1895. Her daughter Jeanie assisted her, as did Robert and Elinor.

Looking back, the pupils in after years thought they had attended a very good school. The mother was patient and understanding, and the soul of enterprise. Robert took the first class in the morning. It was an arithmetic class, but on the blackboard were written each day poems—this was his mother's idea—which the pupils copied and memorized. Elinor White, with brown, sparkling eyes, taught French. Her gentleness and sweetness made this a joyful class, according to the recollection of one who was a pupil. "I have known and learned from many inspiring teachers," says this former pupil, "but the four who made that school are by themselves apart."

Rob and Elinor's engagement lasted about a year. Rob was choosing the road in life he would take, the road on which one would meet love and poetry. Perhaps he made up his mind during a mysterious stay on Ossipee Mountain above the New Hampshire village of Melvin. He took a shack and lived alone for about three months in the summer. Young Robert Frost wanted to think things out. What went through his mind during his retreat? "The thoughts of youth are long, long thoughts," sang the poet Longfellow, and there is no doubt that this summer was a time of long, long thoughts for the young lover. It is also certain that he found his love returned. In late December, 1895, he and Elinor White were married.

Rob had no worldly goods whatever, no economic position, no security. What money he had earned he had given to his mother. "I did not miss it," he has recalled. "Money was

[*42*]

Mother's affair." All he had to give Elinor was himself and a handful of unpublished poems. That was untold wealth to her. The unpublished poems were, after a score of years or so, to see the light of publication, and thereafter to live on indefinitely. When Frost's first book, *A Boy's Will,* appeared in 1913, its readers little guessed that the poems in it had been aging, like good wine, since before his marriage in 1895, and that they had been written before the poet's 22nd birthday. Two other early poems did not appear until *West-Running Brook* came out in 1928. Elinor knew that she was marrying a poet of great promise. Frost wrote other and inferior poems at this time, and it is a curious example of editorial taste that these inferior poems *The Independent* bought and printed. No doubt Robert's pulse beat faster when the mail carrier delivered *The Independent* for August 20, 1896, which contained his poem, "The Birds Do Thus." Later, his liking for this poem cooled and he excluded it from his books. Nor did he care to preserve "Caesar's Lost Transport Ships," in *The Independent* for January 14, 1897, although he must have joyfully reread it many times in the first flush of publication. The September 9, 1897 issue of *The Independent* carried still another youthful poem, "Warning," but it is not in *Complete Poems.*

These appearances in print were encouraging to the young school teacher. Dr. Ward had even lined up some endorsers of the new poet. Bliss Carman, an adviser to Dr. Ward, had approved "My Butterfly," and so had Maurice Thompson, the author of *Alice of Old Vincennes* who wrote of "the extreme beauty of that little ode" and said that it had "some secret of genius between the lines, an appeal to sympathy lying deep in one's sources of tenderness." Still the poet needed all the en-

[43]

couragement Elinor could give him to endure the rebuffs of the next 15 years. Elinor gave up teaching toward the fall of 1896 when she bore a son, Eliot.

Robert taught through the spring of 1897, and then he and Elinor, with their baby, took a house for the summer at Salisbury Point in Massachusetts. Here at last he squarely faced the fact of his chronic lack of money. "It gives me a pang." Maurice Thompson had written Dr. Ward, "to know that its ["My Butterfly"] author is poor. To be a poet and be poor is a terrible lot. What hope is there?" Nevertheless Frost began to hope that there might be a solution to his problem of supporting a family, for clearly he could not dodge family responsibilities now.

With a baby son to provide for, the young father climbed to the attic of the Lawrence house to face the insistent question: What next? He had intended to read the Latin historian Tacitus for a while, but worry about the future kept breaking in. "How was I going to earn a living? All of a sudden it occurred to me: Why couldn't I go to college and become a teacher?"

Spurred by this thought, he sat down on September 11, 1897, and wrote to Dean Briggs of Harvard.

"I desire to enter Harvard this fall, if possible a candidate for a degree from the outset . . . If proficiency in English were any consideration, I make no doubt I could pass an examination in that. You will find verses of my inditing in the current number of the Independent and others better in back numbers. . . . Let me say that if I enter college it must be this year or never. It will be hard if a fellow of my age [23] and general intelligence (!) must be debarred from an education for want of technical knowledge representing less than two months work. All I ask is to be admitted. I don't care how many conditions you encumber me with. . . ."

Harvard let him in. Now he had to make arrangements to cover the costs of going to college. Grandfather Frost said that he would pay the tuition. Elinor's mother took a house in Boston in which the young couple and baby could live.

Rob was old for a freshman when he entered Harvard in the class of 1901. It was unusual then for a college student to be married, so it is not surprising that Rob stood somewhat apart from his class. He did know a brilliant Southerner who sat near him in the Latin class, Waddill Catchings, who became an economist. Frost and Catchings would sometimes walk out in the country and read Terence, the Roman writer of comedies. But students whose names began with "S" sat a long way from the "F's" and Frost never became acquainted with another poet in the class of 1901, Wallace Stevens.

Frost took courses in Latin, Greek, and philosophy. He got high marks in the classics and received a detur, a Harvard honor. The classics were indeed much to Frost's liking, and he found in Virgil's *Eclogues* and *Georgics* the nourishment that his poetic nature most needed. Philosophy lured him in a general way. George Santayana gave a course which he recalls with pleasure in the "golden speech" and the "deliberate speed, majestic instancy" of the exposition of this brilliant thinker whose fame was just beginning.

Frost did not do well in English A, the required freshman course. He was too advanced for it and hated it. Nor did he hit if off with the teacher, Alfred D. Sheffield, who was to be the brother-in-law of the poet T. S. Eliot of the class of 1910. Frost

[45]

did the unconventional thing of turning in a poem, "Now Close the Windows," in place of a daily theme.

"Did you write this for my class?" asked the astonished teacher.

"No."

"So we have published poetry, have we?" said Sheffield in a tone that was unpleasing to Frost.

Here is the poem that left Sheffield cold.

Now close the windows and hush all the fields:
If the trees must, let them silently toss;
No bird is singing now, and if there is,
Be it my loss.

It will be long ere the marshes resume,
It will be long ere the earliest bird:
So close the windows and not hear the wind,
But see all wind-stirred.

In his first year Frost partly worked his way by doing a little teaching in a North Cambridge public school; but in the second year, although he won a big scholarship, nothing went well. Frost recalls that a feeling of suspended animation came over him. "I was restless," he says, "and didn't seem to be liking things again." His mother's school was in difficulty and several times he left Harvard to look after it. But he could not save it. Then he got sick. "So I resigned from the sophomore class at the end of March [1899], to the Dean's regret." But was it really for reasons of health that he quit college a second time? "I know now why," Frost later said. "Harvard had taken me away from the question whether I could write or not."

[46]

It was a time of crisis for him. On April 28, 1899, his daughter Lesley was born in Boston. With two tiny children, Robert and Elinor retired to Methuen to raise chickens. But that was only a makeshift. In the autumn Robert's mother became ill with cancer and went to a sanitarium in New Hampshire. She was only 55. In July of 1900 little Eliot died. That persistent question "What next?" had returned, more insistent than ever.

Through it all Frost was still bewitched by poetry. A man in Windham, New Hampshire, he had known in the interval between Dartmouth and Harvard, a man named Charley Hall, spoke with a racy commonness. The stimulation of his speech had been greater than that of the correct college instructors. On the foundation of this homely, shrewd, living talk, could not poetry be written by a good listener? Could not "talk-songs" be composed? Frost had deserted academic halls for his own peculiar university, a life close to the soil among soil-tinged folk, where he could listen to their turns of thought and feeling and phrase.

Elinor realized that Robert must attend his own one-man university and went to Grandfather Frost who had helped before in spite of his incomprehension. Would he buy them a farm? She told him about a farm they had seen in West Derry, New Hampshire, only 12 miles from Lawrence. A 30-acre farm, not too good, but it had orchard, fields, pasture, woodland, and spring. It was a good enough one-man, one-horse farm. It cost $1,800. Grandfather understood that Robert intended to combine farming and poetry.

When he saw Robert, he asked him: "Shall I give you a year? I know what you are up to. Will you settle down if I give

[47]

you a year to try this out?" This seemed reasonable.

Robert, never one to beg for support, struck the pose of an auctioneer. "Give me twenty, give me twenty!" he dared him.

Still uncomprehending, Grandfather bought the farm for the young couple.

Chapter 6

The Poem That Got a Job

Derry, New Hampshire, was a town of a little over 3,500 population that produced textiles, shoes, and other goods. Today it is nearly twice as big, and it is notable as the place near which Robert Frost farmed and where he taught at Pinkerton Academy.

Frost fitted perfectly into the rolling hills and winding valleys of southeastern New Hampshire, a country of great beauty. Frost's small farm, to which he moved in the fall of 1900, was a couple of miles down the turnpike from the new part of Derry, called the Depot. His white house and connected barn stood on a rise overlooking the famous coach road from Concord, New Hampshire, to Boston, 42 miles to the south.

The Depot was growing fast. It had several shoe factories and was a sprout of the industrial age. But Derry Village had changed scarcely at all since 1880. Here lived Frost's North-of-Boston Yankees who have been described by Reginald L. Cook in *The Dimensions of Frost:* "They have a neighborly love of talk, a notable lack of natural cunning and, on occasion, let go in neurotic outbursts. . . . But when these people have their backs to the wall they can endure what has to be endured." Another friend of Frost's, Cornelius Weygandt, who visited Frost several times in New Hampshire, has said: "All rural New England shares in laconic speech, a picturesqueness of phrase, a stiffness of lip, a quizzicality of attitude, a twistiness of approach to thought, but there is a New Hampshire slant to these qualities."

Derry people were conservative. They regarded their religion and inherited culture with satisfaction. They felt, Frost soon found out, that a satisfactory elevation in education and theology had been achieved before the death of the famous transcendentalist philosopher and poet, Ralph Waldo Emerson, who had died only three years before Robert Frost came to New England. Derry felt that it had only to maintain this level. Like a true New England town, Derry had its academy for just that purpose: Pinkerton Academy stood on a hill overlooking Derry Village.

Frost's farm was separated from his neighbor's farm by a stone wall the poet was later to make famous in "Mending Wall." In the surrounding country a "vanished abode" with only the cellar walls left provided the setting for his "Ghost House." Set well back from the road was the subject of "The Black Cottage."

All was as right for Frost as had been the Lake District for the English poets Wordsworth, Coleridge, and Southey. Frost needed to live in a settled and rooted community that was holding out against the noisy factories overrunning New England. And the academy on the hill was important, too; it was a sign that culture should keep conservatism a little troubled over the larger questions of life lest conservatism fall

[*50*]

into complacency. "I believe in tradition and accident and a bit of an idea bothering tradition," Frost once said. Pinkerton Academy would be in Derry that "bit of an idea."

A month or so after Frost took his farm, his mother, aged only 56, died. But Frost's grandfather lived on. Frost's family grew: a son Carol was born in 1902; a daughter Irma in 1903; another daughter Marjorie in 1905. But by then Robert Frost had shown that he was a failure as a farmer.

At least that was the opinion of folks in Derry. They had laughed at the young farmer who had insisted to a friend that he had learned to be "a real if not a good farmer." How can you be a good farmer, they had scoffed, when you milk your cow at such crazy times as one in the afternoon and twelve at night? But Frost had noted that the cow did not mind so long as the milking was performed at regular intervals. By milking at unusual hours Frost gained the best hours of the night— when other farmers were asleep—for reading and thinking and composing poetry. Robert Frost liked to sleep late and stay up late; the night hours are his creative hours. And so Frost adapted his cow to his temperamental preference for working at night, and did not mind the laughter of his neighbors.

He could not, however, ignore the fat butcher in Derry who was sure by 1905 that Frost was a very poor credit risk. As Frost drove up one spring day to make further purchases on credit, the butcher strode rudely out to the porch of his shop, cocked an appraising eye at Frost's old horse, and indelicately asked if any creditor had a lien, a claim, on him. This made it clear that Frost had to do something besides farm if he was going to feed his family, which with Marjorie's coming numbered six.

Frost has characterized himself as half farmer, half poet, and half teacher—which, by a strange arithmetic, adds up to one poet-sage. And we may ask how Poet Frost had been faring on the living provided by the toil of Farmer Frost? The answer is that Poet Frost had done very well.

Every now and then Frost had made a poem during these five lean years on the farm—good poems, too, that would be praised when his first book appeared in England in 1913. The process of making a poem seems a mysterious one to most people, and indeed poets themselves have not explained it very clearly. Wordsworth, for example, said that a poem "is the spontaneous overflow of powerful feelings; it takes its origin from emotion recollected in tranquillity." This was true enough for Wordsworth, but it was not what happened when Frost made a poem. It was not what happened, for instance, when Frost went through a mown field one day, turning the grass, and came upon a tall tuft of flowers that the mower had spared. His poem, "The Tuft of Flowers," came not from turning to the past and recollecting emotion in tranquillity. "The Tuft of Flowers" came from the present moment.

"A poem," Frost has explained, "begins with a lump in the throat: a homesickness or a love-sickness." So it had been when he had come upon the uncut flowers by the brook. There had been a fresh perception. There had been a disturbing excitement to which the poet had surrendered. There was an impulse—to write a poem. A lump in the throat. "It is a reaching-out toward expression," Frost went on to explain; "an effort to find fulfilment. A complete poem is one where an emotion has found its thought and the thought has found the words."

Yes, Frost had argued, there is a striking resemblance

between the course of a true poem and of a true love. "It [a true poem, a true love] begins in delight, it inclines to the impulse, it assumes direction with the first line laid down, it runs a course of lucky events, and ends in a clarification of life—not necessarily a great clarification . . . but in a momentary stay against confusion. It has denouement. It has an outcome that though unforeseen was predestined from the first image of the original mood—and indeed from the very mood."

So there is a flash of recognition. There is an emotional tension, the lump in the throat that impels a poet to record on paper in verse the details of the moment—as when he recognized the message of the tuft of flowers. He proceeds to write the poem as an act of faith, without foreseeing the outcome. In doing so, the emotion finds its thought, and the thought finds the words. "My definition of poetry," says Frost, "(if I were forced to give one) would be this: words that have become deeds."

"The Tuft of Flowers" did become a deed. "Got me my first real job," Frost has said. "I have never earned a cent except by and through verse. For my first twenty years of it I earned a total of $200. Whole family owe their life to this poem and they'd better believe it."

What happened to change the words of "The Tuft of Flowers" into a deed was this. Frost had made a friend of the minister at Derry, Charles Merriam, who was also a friend of William Hayes Ward and Susan Hayes Ward, his friends of *The Independent*.

"Frost," said Merriam one day, "it's going to be ladies' night at the next meeting of the Derry Village Men's Club. I'd like to put you on the program."

[53]

"Me? How can I entertain the ladies?"

"And the men, too. We want something to appeal to both. We want you to read one of your poems."

"A poem!"

"Yes. That one you showed me last week about the mower who spared some flowers by the brook because he loved them. That's a beautiful poem and I'm sure that some of our visitors will love it. How about reading that one to us?"

"I don't know. I'm shy about reading poetry in public. It's all right in the classroom or at home. But in public—no."

"But your poem sounds so natural. Just read it naturally and you'll feel no embarrassment."

"All right. I'll work up my courage and come."

But Frost had a case of shyness when he looked at the members of the Men's Club and their guests on the meeting night. There were school teachers present who might be critical. When Merriam was ready to introduce him, he handed his manuscript to the minister. "You read it, please," he begged.

Merriam who was practised in public speaking took the sheet of paper and looked at Frost's strong, masculine handwriting. "The Tuft of Flowers," he announced, and then very naturally began to read:

I went to turn the grass once after one
Who mowed it in the dew before the sun.

The dew was gone that made his blade so keen
Before I came to view the leveled scene.

[54]

I looked for him behind an isle of trees;
I listened for his whetstone on the breeze.

But he had gone his way, the grass all mown,
And I must be as he had been,—alone,

'As all must be,' I said within my heart,
'Whether they work together or apart.'

But as I said it, swift there passed me by
On noiseless wings a bewildered butterfly,

Seeking with memories grown dim o'er night
Some resting flower of yesterday's delight.

And once I marked his flight go round and round,
As where some flower lay withering on the ground.

And then he flew as far as eye could see,
And then on tremulous wing came back to me.

I thought of questions that have no reply,
And would have turned to toss the grass to dry;

But he turned first, and led my eye to look
At a tall tuft of flowers beside a brook,

A leaping tongue of bloom the scythe had spared
Beside a reedy brook the scythe had bared.

[55]

The mower in the dew had loved them thus,
By leaving them to flourish, not for us,

Nor yet to draw one thought of ours to him,
But from sheer morning gladness at the brim.

The butterfly and I had lit upon,
Nevertheless, a message from the dawn,

That made me hear the wakening birds around,
And hear his long scythe whispering to the ground,

And feel a spirit kindred to my own;
So that henceforth I worked no more alone;

But glad with him, I worked as with his aid,
And weary, sought at noon with him the shade;

And dreaming, as it were, held brotherly speech
With one whose thought I had not hoped to reach.

'Men work together,' I told him from the heart,
'Whether they work together or apart.'

Hand clapping broke out as Merriam concluded. The school teachers looked at each other and nodded approval. The entire group was moved.

Wouldn't this young farmer Frost make a fine English teacher?—that thought struck the school teachers. Why not plant the idea in the mind of the principal of Pinkerton Acade-

"A leaping tongue of bloom the scythe had spared."

my? And it was done. The idea appealed to the principal who within a short time offered Frost a job.

Thus "The Tuft of Flowers" did in fact rescue Farmer Frost from his failure, and because it did, it is an important deed in the story of Poet Frost.

Chapter 7

New vs. Old at Pinkerton Academy

O ne October morning in 1906 Robert Frost was perplexed as he walked from his farm to the school where he had a part-time appointment to teach English. He was thankful that his hay fever, which had plagued him all summer, had let up. But fresh troubles filled his mind.

He was now a farmer-poet-teacher—a real one, in each occupation. His apple trees earned him more money in a year than he was receiving from teaching; so he wasn't an amateur farmer. He was writing poems, and although they were unpublished, he knew they were good. Good? He knew that "The Death of the Hired Man" was first-rate. And since last spring he had been teaching at Pinkerton Academy. He was now teaching two classes a week at a salary of $200 a year. Very little, of course, but he didn't want a full-time position at $1,-000 a year, which he had been offered.

A poem was at the bottom of his perplexity. Recently *The Independent* had published "The Trial by Existence." He had never expected that any one at Pinkerton Academy would see this poem in print. It was a philosophic poem that said that "the utmost reward of daring should be still to dare," and he thought that it would be over the heads of Pinkerton readers. But he had overlooked the subscription to *The Independent* which the school had taken out. Now he was bothered by the attitude of his fellow teachers. He had written Miss Susan Ward about them.

"I had just begun teaching at Pinkerton Academy when my poem . . . turned up in the school library. Its effect was startling. From the moment of its appearance, all the teachers abruptly broke off all but the most diplomatic relations with me. Put to it for a reason, I thought at first that my poem had led them to question my orthodoxy (if not my sanity). Then I thought that a flock of teachers would be more apt to loathe me for misspelling Derry than for grafting Schopenhauer upon Christianity. Mr. Merriam [the minister at Derry] says that I was twice wrong. I had made myself unpopular by the simple act of neglecting to give Pinkerton the credit for harboring the poet that wrote the poem. It was too funny. But while it lasted and I was still guessing, I was rather miserable. . . ."

This letter oversimplified Robert Frost's disharmony with the teachers at Pinkerton. The truth was that he was bringing a new spirit in education and he was colliding with the old spirit of Pinkerton. A Pinkerton boy when Frost taught there has given in a long letter an inside account of the conflict between new and old that involved Frost.

"There were several fine old teachers, excellent representatives of the school that believed that thoroughness and hard work were the beginning and the conclusion of the educational process." Young Robert Frost believed, however, that school could be exciting. But he was up against an old guard. "Great store was set by Latin which was taught by George W. Bing-

ham, the stern and aged principal, and by Greek in which Mary
Parson, maiden member of a distinguished Derry Village
family, gave instructions. The faculty was true to the good old
Pinkerton tradition. The Academy had been founded in the
first years of the nineteenth century and dedicated to the devel-
opment of cultured Christian character. Old rules governing
the student body were still in effect. Card playing, for example, was forbidden, and for a boy to escort a girl to and from an
entertainment was still a technical violation of 'requirements.'
There were compulsory study hours and compulsory attendance
at church. Students must be in their homes at seven p.m. and
not leave thereafter except on Friday evening when grace was
extended to ten p.m. and Sunday evening when the students
were expected to attend church services. Once a week the principal called the roll of the student body and each student reported his record of the week, thus: 'All the requirements,'
'One exception, excused,' 'Two exceptions.' "

Frost's mother's school had been more progressive than
this, and Frost made no effort to conform to Pinkerton ways.
For a while there was much faculty hostility to Frost. "He did
not," his former student wrote, "arrive at the Academy in time
to participate in the morning chapel exercise; he had no classroom; he defied the Pinkerton tradition in the informality of
his presence and the free-and-easy way he handled his classes.
The fact that he had no college degree would, for a portion of
the faculty, keep him forever outside the circle. He was younger than nearly all the others. A dozen things made him an 'out-
sider.' He looked it and acted it."

Unhappy as this hostility made him, Frost, finishing his
two-mile walk on this decisive October morning, entered the red

brick building with the central tower: his firm jaw showed he was determined that he would not quit. And within a couple of years the old order began to change at Pinkerton, and things began to move in Frost's direction.

Frost was learning about parenthood in these Pinkerton years. He and Elinor were to know grief again in the loss of a child, when Elinor Bettina, born on June 20, 1907, died on the following day.

He was to know, too, the Christmas joys of children. He encouraged his children to write daily in composition books, and on Christmas each year the children gave these books to their parents. The parents made toys for the children. Robert would sit up all night carving little wooden animals to delight his youngsters. "I played with my children more than most fathers," Frost recalls, and he remembers how on one April Fool's Day when spring was late, he made spring flowers out of paper and strewed them on the road. In the evenings he read aloud to his family. He read them Prescott's *History of the Conquest of Mexico,* Melville's *Typee* and *Omoo,* Hakluyt's *Voyages,* the *Odyssey,* Darwin's *Voyage of the Beagle,* and Thoreau's *Walden.* In the summers he took them to Bethlehem in the White Mountains where he hoped to escape from hay fever. He had even written a limerick about hay fever which he told Miss Susan Ward had met with no family applause.

> *There was a poor mortal believer*
> *Who gave way to a thought of hay fever:*
> *He coughed like a cold*
> *Till over he rolled,*
> *And went into the hands of a receiver.*

[*62*]

But the children loved the Lynch farm, and so did Frost. He wrote Miss Ward about "the snug downhill dining room with the view over five ranges of mountains, our talks under the hanging lamp and over the fat blue book, the tea-inspired Mrs. Lynch, baseball, and the blue black Lafayette. There is a pang there that makes poetry. I rather like to gloat over it."

Things were changing at Pinkerton Academy in 1909 when the Frosts came back from Bethlehem. The surprising suggestion had even been made that Robert Frost become principal! He repelled the suggestion with the reminder that he had no college degrees to go after his name.

John Bartlett, a member of the class of 1910, the witness to Frost's collision with the old faculty, also has told what it was like to be a student in one of Robert Frost's classes. He said that in his senior year: "The old order of things at Pinkerton went quickly. A new principal, Ernest L. Silver, came in 1909. There were new teachers and new subjects—agriculture, domestic science, and this and that. Pinkerton in brief time was doing a lot of catching up. I believe that Frost's success with his English classes had a great deal to do with the rapidity and completeness of this change.

"No greater departure from traditional Pinkerton teaching methods could be conceived than those of Robert Frost. A boy of sixteen or seventeen isn't aware in respect to much of a teacher's pedagogy beyond knowing whether it pleases him or not. But, looking back, I believe I know the first great difference between Frost and the other teachers. He had far greater interest in the individual student. He had a way of manifesting this, of asking questions and of making observations in a few words, all the while getting closer to the boy in question. It was

[*63*]

not a professional self-conscious thing, but a desire from Frost's heart to get closer and learn more.

"Late one afternoon as a group of boys were passing a football about on the athletic field, Frost came up. He was a frequent figure on the athletic field and sometimes he would take off his coat and 'make a bluff,' as the boys put it, at playing. This afternoon he happened to come near me. He asked me several questions concerning the Pawtuckaway Mountains where the 'Devil's Den' about which I had written [in a short theme] was located. I answered them awkwardly: I was a shy boy. In a matter-of-fact way he observed that I was a fellow who had ideas.

"That was all there was to the conversation, for a spinning ball came my way, but I can still see Frost and the fall mud and the football bucking machine and the boys on that afternoon. He seemed to show in this conversation several hundred times the interest in me that other teachers had.

"He really had this interest, I am sure, and it was not directed toward me alone, but toward all his students. He asked them personal questions, drew them out.

"In those days Frost was always asking questions of people. Not the mechanical questions of politeness, but questions that would get at things Frost was interested in . . . and he was interested in a great deal. If we took a winter walk toward Londonderry and met a logging team, which we stopped as we came abreast, there would be a conversation right there. Frost would have the teamster talking about logging things and horses and wood roads and such matters. He talked with his students in somewhat the same way. There was always something to be learned from these New Englanders, and Frost learned it. [As he continued to do all his life.]

"And he was interested in the boy's problems of individuality. Seemingly, he could like any sort of boy. He might not win a boy in the first few minutes of his contact with him, but nearly always he won him in the end.

"The most excited boy over an English paper I ever saw was Dave Griffith, the athlete of '10, a magnificent halfback and sprinter. He had written on a sport subject and had earned commendation from Frost. Breaking the study home hour of the dormitory, Dave stealthily went from room to room to announce grandly his accomplishment. Dave had a haughty disregard for scholastic honors in general (few of which he ever received), but he knew when he had something to be proud of.

"We had a boarding student in the Junior class, Arthur Eastman, who was neither among the scholars on one hand nor the athletes on the other. Arthur was suddenly famous for a four-line stanza which Frost was commending to his classes. I believe the boy never again wrote a verse which was praised. On the other hand, one of the older students who turned out verse with great abundance and prided himself on his ability received no approval whatever. The school knew that Frost considered this student's verse of no merit."

Frost remembers his interest in school sports. "At Pinkerton Academy," Frost told me, "I fooled around with the boys on the ballfield and was coach some of the time." He remembers too that the milliner in Derry was married to a famous major league pitcher of the period, the eccentric Rube Waddell. Furthermore, Frost strongly encouraged athletic prowess in his own children. They were tireless walkers, climbed trees, swung on trapezes. The oldest daughter, Lesley, was a runner and skater, so good that she almost qualified for the Olympic skating team later.

"Frost's English classes," Bartlett continued in his reminiscences, "were always 'easy' classes. Frost had none of the taskmaster's attitude, yet his classes did a great deal of work and covered fully as much ground as any ordinary class. Any feeling for literature displayed by a student was cultivated: any talent for writing was nursed along. A few in each class were gradually developed who could always be counted on for lively discussion. Very frequently departures from the regular routine were made. Often, for example, Frost, slumped down in his chair, would read to the class. And every time a new *Critic* was out, Frost would discuss it with his classes.

"The *Critic* was the student publication, and it was better than it had been for many years before Frost's engagement. He let the boys and girls run it largely themselves: faculty supervision of it was much less than formerly. There was a good deal of comradeship between Frost and the *Critic* staff. Unconventional things occurred . . . the *Critic* files may contain at least one poem the distinguished authorship of which is not generally known. I believe the *Critic* sometimes contained, because of his 'hands off' policy, things that he would not have passed for publication. But he knew that his policy was right and held to it.

"He was philosophical, too, when one of the honor members of the Senior class, given liberty in connection with his Commencement essay not in keeping with Pinkerton practice, read a paper at Graduation which was a wretched failure. This boy [Bartlett means himself] had not been required to submit his essay for faculty approval. And he messed the job, actually writing the final paragraphs two hours before he was due on the platform. Frost remarked later, 'It sounded as though you had read one book or article and then written your essay.' That was all that was ever said between us, and it was enough! Frost had divined the fact.

"Out of the English classes came during those years several plays coached by Frost. The plays were a success on both sides of the footlights. Frost liked to have his fun as much as any of the students, and the rehearsals brought us all together in a fine way. These plays were a new thing at Pinkerton. The Academy had presented several of Shakespeare's plays since the century came in but no cognizance of other drama had been taken.

"In 1909 the state began to be interested in Frost's classes. He talked at conventions, booked by Henry Morrison, the New Hampshire State Superintendent. And from time to time educators visited our classes. These convention talks were ordeals, and Frost always came back from them in a condition of exhaustion.

"The student body was with him one hundred per cent as the fall term of 1909 opened. There was a new order of things in the school and Frost was recognized as a big figure.

"I do not recall just when it was that Frost first wrote a formula, famous with his classes, upon a Pinkerton blackboard. He put forward the following kinds of matter used for literary purposes:

Uncommon in experience—uncommon in writing.
Common in experience—common in writing.
Uncommon in experience—common in writing.
Common in experience—uncommon in writing.

The last was the kind of material to search for, he told us.

"We celebrated a football victory over our rival school, Sanborn Seminary, in November, 1909, with a supper provided by the new domestic science department. Frost was the hit of the evening with a string of verses he put on the blackboard. This was one:

In the days of Captain John,
Sanborn Sem had nothing on,
Pinkerton, Pinkerton.

"A few of the boys spent considerable time with Frost out of school hours. I remember a walk over the turnpike to Manchester twelve miles away in the late afternoon, an hour spent in a bookstore, an oyster stew, and then a ride home on the electric railway. Our conversation on walks touched on books only now and then. They might include reminiscences of Frost's early life, discussion of school affairs, aspects of farm life in New Hampshire, some current news happening of importance, and nearly anything else. If in passing a farmhouse the aroma of fried doughnuts came out to us, Frost might propose that we buy some. Down around the corner we might encounter a fern he hadn't seen since he was last in the Lake Willoughby region. And if darkness overtook us and it was a favorable night for observation, Frost would be sure to take at least five minutes to study the heavens and attempt to start our astronomical education." (Stars still fascinate Frost.)

Probably Frost pointed out to the boys his favorite constellation, Canis Major (The Great Dog), to the southeast of Orion. That constellation always made his heart leap, and one night he wrote a joyous poem about it.

> *Canis Major*
> *The great Overdog,*
> *That heavenly beast*
> *With a star in one eye,*
> *Gives a leap in the east.*
>
> *He dances upright*
> *All the way to the west*
> *And never once drops*
> *On his forefeet to rest.*
>
> *I'm a poor underdog,*
> *But tonight I will bark*
> *With the great Overdog*
> *That romps through the dark.*

Bartlett remembered that on these star-gazing walks "there was always plenty of conversation, but almost never any argument. Frost never argued. He knew what he knew, and never had any interest in arguing about it. In the same way he was always willing to let others think what they wanted to think."

Frost enjoyed his supervision of plays at Pinkerton. Within a few weeks in the spring of 1910 Frost produced five plays: Marlowe's *Dr. Faustus*, Milton's *Comus*, Sheridan's *The*

Rivals, Yeats's *The Land of Heart's Desire* and *Cathleen ni Houlihan*—the last two being "modern" at the time. How great a hit Frost made as a play director may be judged by the willingness of old George W. Bingham, the retired pious principal of Pinkerton, to help with the stage properties. The old man stopped Frost on the street after *Dr. Faustus* had been put on and spoke of the next play coming up, *Comus,* which contains licentious scenes in Circe's palace. Would Frost like the use of the communion service of the church for the Circe scenes? the old man wanted to know.

Frost helped Bartlett meet his post-graduation problems. "I remember how I came back to Derry late in 1910," wrote John Bartlett, "having left college 'between two days,' defeated and defiant, meeting disapproval and condemnation. I was a boy getting hit by life and receiving no friendly overtures when I needed them most. Frost heard I was back and walked miles to see me and take me over the country roads for a talk. I remember how a few months later he speeded me on my way to British Columbia with a handshake and a look in the eye. There was a book at that parting, Chesterton's *Heretics.* I read it three times on the way out. I remember letter after letter as I sought a way to fit in at Vancouver, and the frequent letters as I finally started in newspaper work. Letters all about me, my problems. That was what friendship meant to Robert Frost, help to the maximum when a boy needed it."

Chapter 8

Best Teacher in New Hampshire

Robert Frost was well on the road to eminence in education. Henry Morrison, the State Superintendent of Schools, called Frost the best teacher in New Hampshire. But Frost had set his heart on becoming a full-time poet, no matter what other remarkable talents he might have. The Superintendent's praise did not sway him from his goal.

And so it was that Frost whispered to himself, "For one year only," when he put his foot on the next higher rung of the educational ladder. Silver was moving from the headship of Pinkerton to the headship of Plymouth State Normal School, and he invited Frost to come along and teach psychology and the history of education to the young women there. Frost consented to go—at a salary of $1,100, which was higher than his best salary at Pinkerton.

The Frost family had, in fact, begun to pull away from the Derry farm. They had held it for the 10 years required by Grandfather's will before they could take title. Now they were free to sell it, and, after storing their household goods, they put it on the market. On they went to Plymouth in the center of New Hampshire and on the edge of the White Mountains.

Plymouth was an old town. The great statesman and lawyer Daniel Webster had pleaded his first case in its courtroom, and the great novelist Nathaniel Hawthorne had died there. Its teachers' college was the first to be established in New Hampshire, dating back to 1873. It was a good place for a New England poet to live.

Robert loved to walk through the town at nine o'clock of a winter evening and out into the country where he could look at the heavens and see if Sirius the Dog Star was romping. By the time he returned to town, the quiet citizens had, as the city slickers of the period put it, "pulled in the sidewalks" and gone to bed. Frost made a poem out of the difference between the country town at nine o'clock and at ten in the evening.

Good Hours

I had for my winter evening walk—
No one at all with whom to talk,
But I had the cottages in a row
Up to their shining eyes in snow.

And I thought I had the folk within:
I had the sound of a violin;
I had a glimpse through curtain laces
Of youthful forms and youthful faces.

I had such company outward bound.
I went till there were no cottages found.
I turned and repented, but coming back
I saw no window but that was black.

[72]

Over the snow my creaking feet
Disturbed the slumbering village street
Like profanation, by your leave,
At ten o'clock of a winter eve.

At State Normal, Frost was as fresh and original in his teaching as he had been at Pinkerton. The first thing he did was to throw out the old dull volumes of the history of education. Instead he introduced his young women to the works of Plato and Rousseau and other great writers who had been philosophers of education.

"I found that Mr. Frost," said Sidney Cox, a friend Frost made in Plymouth, "was having exciting times teaching psychology, that he wasn't following any chart, but improvising his own courses, and having the girls read real books. He made me interested in Plato's *Republic* and Rousseau's *Emile* when he was in the midst of them with one of his classes. He sometimes mentioned a student who seemed exceptional, but he didn't suppose he was making any great discoveries."

Sidney Cox was from Lewiston, Maine, and he was just down from Bates College to teach English at the high school in Plymouth. There are two stories of how the long friendship between Cox and Frost started. Cox says: "I met Robert Frost in the fall of 1911 at a Normal School dance where both of us were against the wall. The next day he came to the high school to ask me to go for a walk. I went, and when I reached home I had felt from that one talk, as I had never done before, what the real nature of poetry is. After that came many walks, and long casual whole-souled talks. Mr. Frost had no congenial colleagues with whom to walk, and for both of us it was the first, and as it turned out, the only year in Plymouth."

Frost says: "It began one evening in 1911 when we met as strangers looking on at a school dance at Plymouth, New Hampshire, where we were both teachers, he in one school, I in another. I didn't know who he was except that he looked very teasably young. He didn't know who I was except, it seems, that I looked too old. By saying something flippant about the theme papers he had to hurry away to correct I angered him to the point of his inquiring behind my back if it was because of alcohol I had got no further up in the world at my age. I was thirty-seven. I was just teaching psychology in the Plymouth Normal School. He disdained to speak to me on the street for a while afterwards. But his seriousness piqued the mischief in me and I set myself to take him. He came round all right, but it wasn't the last time he had to make allowances for me."

However it started, there ensued one of the longest and truest friendships in Frost's life. Cox, who later became a professor of English at Dartmouth, looked up to Frost as to an admired older brother and treasured the sayings of the poet-teacher. He became a good listener to Frost for the rest of his life and made a book out of his ponderings of Frost's poems and conversation, *A Swinger of Birches,* published after Cox's death in 1952. Frost honored the memory of Cox by dedicating to him in 1962 his book, *In the Clearing,* along with John Bartlett, also deceased, and Louis Untermeyer, still living—three old friends. Untermeyer had edited the Pocket Book collection of Frost's poems.

Cox and Frost took many walks together in that school year of 1911-12. "Perhaps," Sidney Cox recalled, "it was on

[*74*]

the walk at the end of which Mr. Frost treated me at the drug store to the delectable beverage of white grape juice that he first made me realize the absurdity of letting students write compositions on the adventures of a penny, and gave me a realizing sense of the distinction between unconditioned speculation and creative imagination. He didn't put it in any such deadly abstract terms as that. He told me that at Derry he had directed his students to write about what was 'common to experience but uncommon to expression.'

Sidney Cox was invited to Frost's home. "His was a poor man's living room, but there was a bookcase with a lot of attractive books, many of them volumes of poetry—I remember his drawing attention to the exquisite Mosher books [finely printed volumes put out by Thomas Bird Mosher of Portland, Maine]—and there were two or three comfortable chairs. On such evenings the children went to bed and we older ones got comfortable, and Mr. Frost read aloud, or we talked. I suppose two of my favorite plays will always be *Arms and the Man* by Shaw and *The Playboy of the Western World* by Synge because of hearing Mr. Frost read them."

In the spring Cox had to assume the duties of baseball coach at the high school, and "Mr. Frost's lifelong interest in baseball helped me," he has said. "He often talked of players and teams, and once he taught me how to work the short throw to shortstop when there were runners on first and third, and so catch the man stealing home. He was interested in tennis, too, and taught me very clearly what he had recently learned about three different cuts in serving."

All this while Frost was sticking to the pledge he had made to himself in accepting the appointment to the normal school: "For one year only." He had stood at the diverging roads long enough. Now he wanted to plunge wholly and with no other claims on his time into the life of the poet. He was 38 and the "now or never" mood came over him. Moreover, a decision to abandon teaching for three or four years now seemed practicable. Frost had sold his farm and had $1,100 in hand after paying the mortgage. And there was a small income of $800 a year he would get from his grandfather's estate for the next two or three years. He would have to be very economical but freedom to live for and by poetry for a few years was at last possible. For a while he thought of moving to Vancouver, British Columbia, where John Bartlett, his former student at Pinkerton, was doing quite well for himself; and he corresponded with his former pupil on living conditions in Vancouver. He heard that living costs were high there, and England was discussed as an alternative.

One day, Mrs. Frost, standing at the ironing board in the kitchen at Plymouth, settled the choice for England. "Yes," she cried, "let's go over there and live under thatch."

Preparations began at once. Frost told Silver, his principal and educational benefactor. Silver was aghast at what seemed to him a casual giving up of a good school job and the uprooting of four children.

"You can never come back to this school if you leave now," he felt obliged to tell Frost.

"Silver felt that I was going to Hell," Frost said. "He couldn't get it at all."

Frost persisted, and went on to Boston ahead of the family to buy the steamship tickets. They cost $60 apiece for Robert and Elinor; the children went free.

Although puzzled, Silver was kind, and helped to put Mrs. Frost and the children on the train for Boston. At this time Frost had not written his poem, "The Road Not Taken," but its last lines are appropriate to his voyage to England in September of 1912.

> Two roads diverged in a wood, and I—
> I took the one less traveled by,
> And that has made all the difference.

In the hold of the *Parisian* traveled Elinor's rocking chair and Robert's own Morris chair, which was just right to support a shelf he used as a writing-board, both neatly crated for the trip. Robert Frost thought he would be gone at least for three or four years, and he wanted some of his household effects in the new home.

Chapter 9

The Mysterious Publisher and Discoverer Ezra Pound

On September 15, 1912, Robert Frost wrote a letter from his new home in England to his old friend, Miss Susan Ward. He had taken a small house at Beaconsfield, Buckinghamshire:

"Here we are," he wrote, "between high hedges of laurel and red-osier dogwood, within a mile or two of where Milton finished Paradise Lost on the one hand and a mile or two of where Gray lies buried on the other. . . . To London town what is it but a run? Indeed when I leave writing this and go into the front yard for a last look at earth and sky before I go to sleep, I shall be able to see the not very distant lights of London flaring like a dreary dawn."

A former policeman had sent Frost to this little haven. Knowing nothing of England and nothing of its literary life, Frost had gone to the office of *T. P.'s Weekly* on his second morning in London and asked to see the man who wrote the "Country Walks" department. He thought that this man could tell him about country cottages for rent near London. The "Country Walks" columnist, it turned out, had been a London "bobbie," and was quite experienced in giving directions to strangers. He had been able to direct Frost to the right place for him. London bobbies answer many odd queries.

And so, Frost had brought his family to The Bungalow, Beaconsfield, along with the furniture he had shipped from America.

After 20 years of submitting poetry to American magazines, he had become completely discouraged about his prospects of recognition in his native land. On this September evening he told his disappointment to Miss Ward:

"But in any case I should not stay [in America], if only for scorn of scorn—scorn of the scorn that leaves me still unnoticed among the least of the versifiers that stop a gap in the magazines. The Forum gives me space for one poem this year; the [Youth's] Companion for two. The Independent, longest my friend, has held one of my poems unprinted now these three years. So slight is my consideration."

In 20 years he had had only 14 poems published. And yet, as he arranged his manuscripts at Beaconsfield, he found he had written enough poems to make nearly four books. And he knew that they were good, too. That was why he had taken the gamble of resigning from a teaching career and staking everything on them.

And indeed the magazine situation in America had been bad for poets. Once a year Frost had sent packets of poems to *Scribner's, The Atlantic Monthly, The Century* and other strongholds of literary culture, and they had always come back. He had finally placed some poems in *The Youth's Companion,* but the editor, Mark A. de Wolfe Howe, had stretched his policy to let Frost's adult poems in. Ironically, this arid period for young poets was just ending as Frost sailed for England. In October, 1912 appeared the first issue of *Poetry* magazine, in Chicago, edited by Harriet Monroe, and this heralded a more hospitable time for new poets. Even so the first group of poems which Frost sent to *Poetry* from England was returned to him.

The English literary scene before World War I was more exciting than the American but Frost did not know this. So unknowing was he that after he had sorted out the 30 poems that make up his first book and set out to find a publisher, he knew no one to ask for advice but the same former policeman who had found his Beaconsfield cottage for him. Ruling out the big publishers, Frost asked the *T. P.'s Weekly* expert on country walks if he could recommend a small publisher for poetry.

The former policeman said: "Little books like that cost the author about fifteen pounds."

"But I will never publish a book at my own expense," stoutly declared Frost.

"How about Elkin Matthews then?" proposed the rural walks expert.

"He's a vanity publisher," objected Frost, meaning that Elkin Matthews was known to take subsidies from poets for printing their works. This was partly true. Sometimes, as with Ezra Pound, Matthews lost his commercial head, and paid the printing costs himself.

"Maybe David Nutt would be the firm for you," offered Frost's adviser.

"David Nutt? Didn't he publish a book by W. E. Henley? That might be the place." Henley, the poet of "Invictus," the crippled giant upon whom Robert Louis Stevenson had modeled Long John Silver in *Treasure Island*—the firm that published him might indeed by the very place. Robert Frost went off to the David Nutt office at 17 Grape Street.

He was told that he could not see David Nutt that day but could if he returned the following day. He did and met "a strange lugubrious lady, a Frenchwoman," dressed in "deep black weeds," who said to him: "I will speak for David Nutt." This was a deep mystery, for Frost did now know that David Nutt had been dead for several years and that his son David had died of drowning. The strange Frenchwoman was his widow, but this Frost could not guess. Nevertheless he left the manuscript—30 poems typed out by his daughter Lesley on his old Blickensderfer—with the lugubrious representative of David Nutt.

Three days later—a remarkably short time for manuscript consideration—he received a card inviting him to call at David Nutt's. His book was accepted!

The widow, however, showed no enthusiasm for the book she was accepting. She expressed no feeling of any kind nor did she give any inkling of why she was taking it. Had she an adviser who had at once recognized that here was an important new poet and told her with the excitement of a discoverer that she must surely publish him? She made no mention of any adviser, and to this day we do not know by what considerations she was moved to accept Frost's sheaf of poems. She confined herself strictly to business. Here was a contract which Frost read far enough to see that it was on a royalty basis and not a subsidy arrangement. It did not offer an advance payment against royalties, which authors like, but it did offer, Frost noted, a royalty rate of twelve and a half per cent on each copy sold. And it stipulated that he should give his future books to David Nutt. This gave him misgivings but after thinking it over, he signed the paper shortly before Christmas of 1912. It would have been nice if there had been an advance with which to splurge a bit on Christmas presents. Oh well, it was enough to get published at the publisher's expense.

Most publishers try to launch their authors into the current of literary life, but not Mrs. Nutt. She introduced Frost to no one in literary circles, and when he visited London, he walked about the city in loneliness. By himself, he found the way into English literary life in an amusing way. One dark winter morning of 1912–13 Frost noticed that a new book shop was about to open on Devonshire Street. A clerk was dressing the window with new books of verse, broadsides and photographs, and had put up a notice that Harold Munro's Poetry Book Shop would open that very evening. The lonely American went in and asked if he might attend the meeting.

"The guests are invited," said the clerk, "but you might try to get in just the same."

That evening an uninvited guest sat on the stairway listening to a reading by John Drinkwater.

"I see by your shoes that you are an American," said the young man sitting a step below him. This was F. S. Flint, a British civil servant who was one of the new group of Imagist poets, poets who wrote to unrhymed cadences and made sharp, clear images.

Frost owned up to his nationality, and confessed to writing poetry.

"Do you know your countryman Ezra Pound?"

"No," said Frost. "I have never heard of him."

"Well, you should know him. But, for heaven's sake, don't let him know that you never heard of him."

[*83*]

Flint did speak to Pound and a few days later Frost received at Beaconsfield a card that read:

Ezra Pound, Number Five Church Walk, London. At home sometimes.

The man who sent this card had been born in Idaho, attended the University of Pennsylvania and Hamilton College, and gone abroad in 1907 where he was becoming as famous an expatriate as the painter Whistler had been. He was a rebel against poetic conventions and was assuming leadership in London of a new school of poets. Frost took his time about an-

Belatedly, Robert Frost called on Ezra Pound.

swering the invitation. As he tells it, "one day, maybe in March, finding myself in Kensington near a sign 'Church Walk' I pulled out the card from my vest pocket and knocked at the door."

It was a fateful meeting for both men: fateful for Frost because he was to gain the first influential critic for his poetry; fateful for Pound because he was to have in Frost many years later a very influential intercessor for his release from a mental institution.

Frost interrupted Pound taking a bath. The flamboyant young American with a slight beard—some said that he was trying to look like Shakespeare—donned an ornate Oriental dressing gown and expressed annoyance that his caller had been slow in answering his summons. Almost at once he extracted from Frost the news that David Nutt was publishing his book.

"Is the book out?"

"No," said Frost. "I know nothing about it."

"We'll go over to the press and get an advance copy," Pound announced grandly, and over to the David Nutt office the two went. There was an advance copy available, "and Pound (not I)," says Frost, "took possession of the first copy of my book. I had to walk back to his lodgings with *him* holding *my* book."

Back at 5 Church Walk, Pound began reading the book, while Frost stood around impatiently. Presently Pound said: "You don't mind *our* liking this?"

"Oh no—go ahead and like it."

"You'd better find a book to read," Pound said, taking an even firmer clutch on Frost's book. After a while he said: "I guess you'd better run along. I'm going to review your book."

[*85*]

Almost at once Pound wrote to Alice Corbin, assistant editor of the new Chicago magazine, *Poetry:* "Have just discovered another Amur'kn [Robert Frost]. VURRY Amur'k'n with, I think, the seeds of grace. Have reviewed an advance copy of his book, but have run it too long. Will send it as soon as I've tried to condense it."

This was the beginning of public recognition of Frost by leaders of critical opinion.

Pound, who was given to discovering "finds," had a new "find" and showed Frost the literary life of London. He took him to luncheons, studios and parties, among them the subsequently famous Tuesday evenings at T. E. Hulme's, philosopher and Imagist poet. He gave him his own books of verse —*Personae* and *Ripostes*—which Frost told him he liked, and Pound replied: "If you value them. . . . But it's all old stuff. I shall not go back to it."

So Frost became a caller at Pound's flat in which "books were everywhere; old leather trunks bulged with them, the limp, wire-cloth couch seat was held up by dusty tomes shoved underneath." Here Pound would tell his friends—Frost and some others—that they were expected at tea—at May Sinclair's, to take an actual example—and off the little procession would go, Pound striding at its head, "tall, fair-skinned, blond, clothed in black with black, flat-rimmed hat, carrying a long, gold-headed cane." Frost was described by a fellow guest on the May Sinclair occasion as "dignified, a little shabby, almost a small town schoolmaster, but much too awake and smart."

In this manner Frost, for the only time in his life, went about in literary circles—and loved it. He was out of his isolation at last.

Chapter 10

Welcome to the Ranks of Poets

O ne thing about the mysterious Mrs. Nutt: she acted with speed. It had taken her only three days to accept *A Boy's Will* and only three months to publish it. As a rule, publishers require several weeks to reach a decision and at least six months to publish. But on a day in April of 1913 Robert Frost was fondling, as is the way of young authors, one of his own copies of his first book, a small volume bound in flexible brown pebbled cloth with *A Boy's Will* lettered in gold on the front cover. After 20 years he at last had a book out—not a "vanity" book he was paying for but a book printed at the publisher's expense and offered to the public at a price of one shilling six-pence. He could not help remembering that when his grandfather had said to take a year for poetry, he had replied: "Give me twenty."

He had certainly met a lot of poets lately. In America he had met poetry-lovers but never a poet; now he knew a dozen. Sometimes he had been disappointed. Pound had introduced him, to William Butler Yeats, the leader of the Irish literary renaissance. Back at Pinkerton Frost had put on two plays by Yeats; he was prepared to like him. But somehow they had not

[*87*]

hit it off together. Pound had also had Frost meet an influential ex-editor Ford Madox Hueffer, who later changed his name to Ford Madox Ford. Hueffer, who wrote verse, had been editor of *The English Review,* one of the two best literary magazines in England.

Pound had indeed been generous in introducing Frost; but Frost, on his own, had been making friends, and liking them rather better than the aesthetic company Pound kept. Frost's own new friends were called the Georgian poets. He had come to know the man who was at the very center of this group —Harold Monro, proprietor of the Poetry Book Shop where F. S. Flint had noticed his American shoes. Monro, himself a poet, edited a review, *Poetry and Drama,* for the Georgian poets as well as producing anthologies of their poetry. It was quite natural that Frost should be drawn toward these poets, for the Georgians, hating the ugliness of industrialism, were trying to write a poetry of rural life. They were trying to do something else that Frost liked: to bring the language of everyday speech into their verse.

Frost preferred the Georgians—Lascelles Abercrombie, Wilfrid Gibson, and Edward Thomas, especially Thomas—to the Ezra Pound circle who met at T. E. Hulme's flat. At Hulme's, free verse of the Imagist variety was the vogue but free verse did not appeal to Frost. It was like playing tennis with the net down, he said.

The Imagists believed in thriftiness with words. To illustrate this cult of strict economy, Pound cut out two words from one of Frost's poems.

"You've done it in fifty words," he said. "I've shortened it to forty-eight."

"And spoiled my metre, my idiom and idea," answered Frost. That was what he meant by playing with the net down.

Thereafter Pound, who loved to teach, passed the word around not to try to change Frost. "He's set in his ways."

This private recognition is enjoyable, Frost was thinking, as he turned the pages of his freshly printed copy of *A Boy's Will,* but what will the reviewers say? In his later life Frost has professed to care little about reviewers, but in early April, 1913 there was a tingle of expectancy as he waited to hear their opinions. He had not long to wait.

On April 5 in the London *Athenaeum* appeared the first review—unsigned but insiders knew it was by Frost's new friend, Edward Thomas. It was favorable and was soon followed by other favorable reviews: in the *Times Literary Supplement, Poetry and Drama,* the London *Bookman,* the *Nation,* and the *English Review.* The review in the last, in June, 1913, was by the British novelist Norman Douglas, of *South Wind* fame.

Douglas declared that "it does one good to glance awhile into the simple woodland philosophy of Mr. Frost," and one may imagine Frost grunting at the adjective "simple" and saying under his breath: "Simple? Just you wait until you have read more of the opposites I contain in my poetry." But Douglas said the right thing when he called the book "an image of things really heard and seen. There is a wild, racy flavor in his poems; they sound that *inevitable* response to nature which is the hall-mark of true lyric feeling."

Pound was saying something similar but at greater length in his review of *A Boy's Will* in the Chicago magazine, *Poetry* —Frost's first American review. The book, Pound wrote, "has the tang of the New Hampshire woods. . . . This man has the good sense to speak naturally and to paint the thing, the thing as he sees it . . . One reads the book for the 'tone,' which is homely, by intent, and pleasing, never doubting that it comes direct from his own life, and that no two lives are the same. . . . He is without sham and without affectation."

But the crowning review came late—on September 15 in the *Academy*—an open-hearted welcome of Frost to the ranks of born poets. It beautifully summed up the general response to *A Boy's Will*. "The poems combine, with a rare sufficiency," said the anonymous *Academy* reviewer, "the essential qualities of inevitability and surprise. We have read every line with that amazement and delight which were too seldom evoked by books of modern verse . . . it is undoubtedly the work of a true poet. We do not need to be told that the poet is a young man; the dew and the ecstasy—the audacity, too—of pristine vision are here. . . . It is extraordinarily free from a young poet's extravagances [the reviewer did not, of course, know that Frost was thirty-nine] . . . it is so simple, lucid and experimental that, reading a poem, one can see clearly with the poet's own swift eyes. . . . One feels that this man has *seen* and *felt:* seen with a revelatory, a creative vision; felt personally and intensely; and he simply writes down, without confusion or affectation, the results thereof. . . . No one who really cares for poetry should miss this little book."

These were words that vindicated Frost's stubborn faith in his poetry, maintained through 20 years of neglect. It was sweet confirmation of his belief in himself to read: "We have not the slightest idea who Mr. Robert Frost may be, but we welcome him unhesitatingly to the ranks of poets born . . . he should presently give us work far worthier of honor than much which passes for front-rank poetry at the present time."

Such reviews made sweet music to publisher as well as to poet. Convinced that she had a fine poet on her list, Mrs. Nutt went after Frost for a second volume. Frost had been revising a number of what he called "talk poems," and Lesley had been typing them for submission. He was ready to sign a new contract with David Nutt, and that firm announced that it would publish in 1914 a new book by their new poet. The book appeared with the title: *North of Boston.*

It was reassuring to have a publisher who wanted to bring out a second book. If only David Nutt would give some sales accounting and pay the royalties that had accumulated.

Frost headed the letter "The Bungalow, Beaconsfield, Bucks, Eng." and dated it "October 28, 1913." He was bringing his friend, Thomas Bird Mosher of Portland, Maine, up to date. "I give you fair warning," he wrote, "I am going to have my moderate success in these islands." He paused in recollection and then wrote: "Binyon had me to lunch the other day with Bridges." Mention of Binyon brought back memory of Frost's being rescued from drowning in the summer just past.

Frost had taken his family to a lonely fishing village, King's Barn, in Scotland and there had met a Scottish scholar named E. C. Smith. Bathing in the Firth of Forth, Frost had been carried too far from shore but Smith had quickly organized a chain of rescuers and fetched him to safety. Some time later Smith had introduced him to Lawrence Binyon, English poet, dramatist, and writer on Oriental art. Binyon, like many other English poets, had taken to the American poet at once, and now he had brought Frost to meet no less a literary personage than Robert Bridges who had just been appointed Poet Laureate of England. "A fine old boy," Frost thought him, "with the highest opinion of his opinions."

Frost did not care for Bridges' fondness for a theory of quantitative verse. The idea that syllables in English have fixed quantity as syllables in a dead language like Latin have fixed length was not at all to Frost's taste. "The living part of a poem," he had stoutly asserted against Bridges, "is the intonation entangled somehow in the syntax, idiom and meaning of a sentence." He must write his friend Sidney Cox about this matter of words existing in the mouth, not in books; he must work out his own theory of "the sound of sense." Meanwhile he must tell Mosher about his plans to move further into the country.

"When I can get rid of this house I am to go to Gloucester to live, to be with Wilfrid Gibson and Abercrombie. I am out with Pound pretty much altogether. . . ." It was of the Georgian poets Frost was thinking as he concluded his letter to Thomas Bird Mosher. "These Englishmen are very charming. I begin to think I shall stay with them till I'm deported. If I weren't so poor I should plan to stay five years anyway."

That was the trouble. His capital was getting lower every month and very little money came in from an occasional sale of a poem to a magazine; from David Nutt no royalties came. Nevertheless he and Elinor Frost had the feeling that 1914 would be a big year in their lives, and the children caught this feeling. Lesley wrote on the cover of the composition book in which the children would write their thoughts during the coming twelve months:

An Important Year.
by
Four Children.
Dedicated
To
Papa and Mamma.

This important year began when suddenly Frost wrote
a new poem, "Birches." It became one of his most beloved
poems. Then Lesley finished typing the poems—the eclogues
or short pastoral dialogues—that would make up his second
book, *North of Boston*. He turned it in to Mrs. Nutt. That dour
lady had seemed jealous of the small sums Frost had been sent
by magazines. She thought that he had no right under his contract with her, which was indeed a one-sided contract, to sell .
any of his poems before delivering the book manuscript to her.

At last the Frosts gave up their Beaconsfield bungalow
and moved into London for one glorious week. Frost had sold
some poetry to Harold Monro's magazine, *Poetry and Drama,*
and was paid off with rooms on the upper floor of Monro's
Poetry Book Shop. Here W. W. Gibson had had a room and
here the sculptor Jacob Epstein was living at the very time Frost
stayed there. After London it was on to the border of Gloucestershire and Herefordshire, well over toward Wales.

It was "walking country" that Frost had moved to, just
right for a man who loved to walk and botanize or at night to
look at the stars. It was a rich pastoral country of slow streams,
red marl, and low hills. A small river, a tributary of the Severn,
ran through it, and an isolated 100-foot eminence, May Hill,
dominated it. There was plenty of woodland.

[*93*]

Lascelles Abercrombie had a small thatched cottage there near Dymock, Gloucestershire. Two or three years later Wilfrid Gibson took a cottage at The Greenway, two miles away; it had the picturesque name of The Old Nailshop. Frost liked Gibson, who took his subjects from common life and became known as "the poet of the industrial poor." Gibson had looked around and found Little Iddens for Frost, a real farmer's house, two miles from The Old Nailshop. Little Iddens was a small, half-timbered cottage adjoining a farm. It was flanked by a little orchard in which Frost liked to sit and talk and look at May Hill six miles away. This was cider country as well as walking country, and Frost kept a barrel of cider at hand for visitors and for hired help. He explained in a letter to Sidney Cox that no cider barrel meant no visitors and no hired help.

This was a sunny time in the life of Frost, and he expanded in the warm company of his English friends. Twelve years later Gibson commemorated this spring and summer in a glowing poem, "The Golden Room." He told how in the lamp-lit living room, he and the Frosts, Abercrombie, Rupert Brooke, and the Thomases talked and laughed. Frost did much of the talking. His New England speech and jests and turns of phrase delighted them.

Of the group, Edward Thomas had become a great friend. In fact, Frost later said "the closest I ever came in friendship to anyone in England or anywhere else in the world I think was with Edward Thomas . . . 1914 was our year. I never had, I never shall have another such year of friendship."

Frost's children were entranced by Thomas, a London-bred essayist and journalist of Welsh descent who had left home early to become versed, as Frost had, in country things. He was a tall, fair-haired, sensitive man who had endured poverty to follow a writing career. He was just the man to match Frost's devotion to nature. Frost discovered beneath his friend's prose the stuff of poetry and showed him how to release it.

April 18, 1914 was a red letter day in this important year, for on that day David Nutt published *North of Boston*. Among the dramatic narratives that would soon become favorites of the poetry-reading public were "Mending Wall," "The Death of the Hired Man," "Home Burial," and "After Apple-Picking." The lyrics in *A Boy's Will* had been well received but *North of Boston* was greeted with almost a unanimous chorus of praise. The *Times Literary Supplement* of London, usually quite restrained in comment on American writers, declared at once that "poetry burns up out of [*North of Boston*], as when a faint wind breathes upon smouldering embers."

Edward Thomas took three reviews to say all he thought about the new book. In the *Daily News* he affirmed that "this is one of the most revolutionary books of modern times, but one of the quietest and least aggressive. It speaks, and it is poetry." He went on to say in *The English Review* that *North of Boston* presents "a unique type of eclogue, homely, racy, and touched by a spirit that might, under other circumstances, have made pure lyric on the one hand or drama on the other." He had one more go at the book in *The New Weekly* where he said that Frost possessed "a kind of healthy, natural delicacy like Wordsworth's" which would be not the last time that critics would think of Frost and Wordsworth as of equal rank.

In *The Nation* (London) Lascelles Abercrombie, like Edward Thomas, stressed "the sound of sense" that Frost's new book had; "it is, in fact," Abercrombie said, "poetry composed, as far as possible, in a language of *things*. . . . [Frost] seems trying to capture and hold within metrical patterns the very tones of speech—the rise and fall, the stressed pauses and little hurries, of spoken language."

It was most gratifying to Frost to hear from the critics that far from finding his poetry flat and prosaic, as might have been feared, they were finding it full of the delightful "sound of sense." But just what does the "sound of sense" mean? No one has ever bettered Frost's own explanation. He once wrote on a blackboard a primer version of sense:

> I see a dog.
> The dog is in the house.
> I will put him out.
> He will come back.

There it is, four lines, nineteen words, that make sense but are uninteresting, dramatic, unpoetic in sound. Now let us put this sense into tones of voice:

> There's that dog again.
> Get out of here, you brute!
> Oh, what's the use! He'll come back.

Here are compression and energy, changes of feeling and drama. The words have come alive . . . words charged with tone can be taken up by poetry.

In *The Bookman* Wilfrid Wilson Gibson repeated what Frost's other poet-friends had been saying. Gibson had enjoyed joshing Frost about his native land, but now Frost was able to turn the tables. Gibson's poetry had a certain following in the United States and aroused American readers to write him notes of appreciation. These notes, however, sometimes began "Dear Bro." and proceeded to give other signs in spelling and grammar of semiliteracy and raw taste, and it was these "Dear Bro." letters that Gibson delighted to twit Frost about. Now Frost received his first letter from an American admirer. It was on stationery of fine quality from Four Winds Farm, Stowe, Vermont. The neat script informed him that the writer and her mother had enjoyed his poetry. The signature was that of a Mrs. Holt. "This," said Frost triumphantly to Gibson, "is the kind of reader I have in America." But he did not suspect that this reader of taste was the wife of the well-known publisher, Henry Holt.

August 4, 1914, was the black letter day of this important year that changed Frost's life and eventually caused him to cut short his stay in England. It was the day that England, reacting to the German violation of Belgium, declared war on Germany. Rupert Brooke quickly enlisted, and Edward Thomas soon felt the need to join up. Frost thoroughly sympathized with England's cause but was unpleasantly startled to find that some of his rustic neighbors were suspicious of him. Wasn't his New England accent ground for suspicion? And what about the way he came and went without explanation? He might be a German!

Then he had a disagreeable conversation with Mrs. Nutt, who invited him and Elinor to dinner, a long delayed token of interest in her author. Frost quite naturally inquired how his book was doing and was taken aback when the lady resented his inquiry.

"Just like you Americans—all dollar chasers!" she charged.

"But, Mrs. Nutt," Frost innocently answered, "I am not

[97]

asking about the money—I only want to know if people like the book."

"Dollar chasers!" the shilling-squeezing widow shot back.

"If you call me a dollar chaser," Frost said with an attempt at humor, "I'll go home and keep America out of the war!"

As Frost wrote his friend Sidney Cox, "The war is an ill wind to me. It ends for the time being the thought of publishing any more books. Our game is up. . . . So we may be coming home if we can find the fare or a job to pay the fare after we get there."

Nevertheless Frost stayed on for months. He gave up Little Iddens and the Frosts moved into The Gallows with the Abercrombies, thus cutting down on expenses for both families. At last Elinor Frost had her wish to live under thatch fulfilled, but the black shadow of war lay over everything.

In December Frost had word that an American publisher was importing copies of his book from Nutt. "It turns out," he wrote Thomas Bird Mosher, "that my American publisher is Henry Holt. . . . I don't know how it came about unless it was through someone of the name of Holt who wrote me an appreciative letter from Stowe Vermont in the summer."

But what to do about returning to America? Had German submarines made the whole Atlantic Ocean unsafe? Wouldn't travel across the ocean become more dangerous, the longer he waited? Did he dare to stay on with his family in England?

The year 1915 came in and people knew now that it would be a long war. Early in February Frost made the decision to take his family back to New England. He engaged passage on the *St. Paul*, sailing from Liverpool on February 13.

Chapter 11

Greetings from Amy Lowell and Henry Holt

Adelightful surprise awaited Robert Frost in New York. But ignorant of the change in his prospects that was so near, the poet was a very anxious father as the *St. Paul* ploughed across the Atlantic. He had written Sidney Cox that he knew *North of Boston* was "epoch making. . . . All I ask now is to be allowed to live." The crossing was dangerous. While the Frosts were at sea, Germany officially declared a submarine blockade of Great Britain. The *St. Paul* crew blacked out the portholes and conducted lifeboat drills.

Elinor and Robert anxiously discussed what they should do in America. They had stretched their money—only $3,600 —over two and a half years in England. It was gone now, but perhaps there was still some money in Grandfather Frost's estate. Robert must make a trip to Lawrence to find out. In spite of his English success, Robert had not yet found a market for his poems in America. Only that new *Poetry* magazine that Harriet Monroe edited had bought anything he had offered. He knew that David Nutt had made some sort of arrangement to send an American publisher some copies of *North of Boston,* but when had David Nutt ever disclosed to him its dealings or paid him even a farthing on its sales? Nevertheless he and Elinor decided that somehow they would manage to buy a farm at Franconia in New Hampshire and raise vegetables for their own table.

There was still another problem. The Frosts were bringing to refuge in America the oldest son of their great friend Edward Thomas, who had once thought he might emigrate to New Hampshire to live near them. Farewell to that dream. Instead Thomas was enlisting in the British Army and entrusting 15-year-old Mervyn to Frost.

The tête d'armée *landed in New York and found he was famous.*

On Washington's Birthday the *St. Paul* steamed into New York harbor, and immigration officials boarded her. The Mervyn Thomas problem was immediately aggravated. The boy was slightly under 16 years and could not therefore be admitted. He would have to be detained on Ellis Island until he could be deported to England. To cap the rejection, Uncle Sam was not welcoming an underage son of an English poet-soldier when the sponsor, like Frost, had no substantial bank balance to guarantee that the boy wouldn't become a public charge. Thus, before the Frosts came down the gangplank, Mervyn was separated from them. A bad omen!

It was a bleak day. The family, from nine-year-old Marjorie to the 40-year-old father carrying hand luggage, set out to walk uptown. No one remembers what the plan was. The oldest daughter Lesley thinks that it was to take the Fall River boat in the evening, the cheapest way to cover the first leg of a trip to New Hampshire. A friend of the family thinks the plan was to walk over to the East Side and there take the elevated to Grand Central Terminal and camp in its waiting room the rest of the day.

Whatever the plan was, it was changed when Robert Frost —*Tête d'armée* (head of an army), as Lascelles Abercrombie used to call him at Little Iddens—halted his little band at a newsstand on a side street. He had noticed on the stand a new magazine, *The New Republic,* which he had heard about but had never seen. The magazine seemed to be staring at him because on the cover was the announcement of a review of his new book by Amy Lowell. The magazine was quickly purchased and its pages flipped to Amy Lowell's long review.

Miss Lowell, a power in reviewing circles, said that she

had heard of Frost when she had been in England in the summer of 1914. He was, she explained, an expatriate only in a physical sense. Frost's eye took in rapidly her statement that "Living in England he is, nevertheless, saturated with New England" and skipped on to "most American volume of poetry which has appeared for some time." But what was this Boston Brahmin woman saying—he had no sense of humor! Well, never mind; the eye danced on to a description of his subject-matter: "it is a latter-day New England, where a civilization is decaying to give place to another and very different one. . . . the book is an epitome of a decaying New England." That made him demur, but Miss Lowell closed with warm praise. "He tells you what he has seen exactly as he has seen it. And in the word *exactly* lies the half of his talent. The other half is a great and beautiful simplicity of phrase . . . a book of unusual power and sincerity."

The elated Frost, according to one biographer, marched immediately to the office of Henry Holt & Co. Frost told another biographer he went the next day. No matter. Frost knew the importance of this recognition. *The New Republic* was already an influential magazine, and Amy Lowell, sister of the president of Harvard University, wealthy, and herself a poet, was an influential herald of new poets. It was delightful to know that *North of Boston* was actually out in the bookstores in America. So he made his way to Holt's and there met Alfred Harcourt, the manager of the trade book department.

Harcourt explained how American publication had come about. The Mrs. Holt who had written Frost in England was the wife of his boss, Henry Holt. She had sent an English copy of *North of Boston* with a letter of recommendation to Har-

[*102*]

court—and he had tossed the book and letter into the waste-basket; he knew the literary whims of the wives of bosses. But later something had led him to take a look at the rejected book, and he opened his eyes wide. He knew just the Vermont author—Dorothy Canfield Fisher—to read this book, and he sent it to her. Back came word that he should certainly publish this new poet Frost. And so Holt had imported a small edition of 150 copies from Mrs. Nutt and distributed it.

What a time they had had with that woman! She had made them pay a stiff price and had been very difficult about American rights. Moreover, she had done nothing about an American copyright. Well, Holt had decided that she had treated Frost unfairly, binding him to give her five books, yet never making an accounting of royalties; so Holt had just gone ahead and printed a first American edition of *North of Boston*. Harcourt had told Harrison Smith and Sinclair Lewis who were also in the publishing business that Holt would sell ten thousand copies of *North of Boston* the first season.

Harcourt had shown Francis Hackett, the literary editor of *The New Republic,* the advance proofs of *North of Boston,* and Hackett had picked "The Death of the Hired Man" to appear in *The New Republic* two weeks earlier. Here was a check for Frost for $90 in payment.

This was delightfully flabbergasting. It meant that Frost could telegraph the Lynches in Bethlehem, New Hampshire, and send his family there. So Elinor and the children were dispatched to them while Robert busied himself with the release of Mervyn Thomas. Young Thomas, he found, was having a most unpleasant time on Ellis Island. He had been herded in with some rough characters, one of whom committed suicide the first night. The immigration examiners looked into the case of the frightened youth and decided that he must be sent back to England. In desperation Frost appealed to his new friend, Alfred Harcourt, who secured the aid of a brilliant, well-known lawyer, Charles C. Burlingham. Burlingham promptly gave Frost a letter to Frederic C. Howe, Immigration Commissioner. Howe acted at once to release Mervyn to the custody of Robert Frost, who now had standing as a sudden celebrity in the literary world. Frost was able to send Mervyn on to English friends of Edward Thomas who were staying in New England.

Early in March Frost reached his old home town, Lawrence, and looked into his grandfather's estate. It took a little time to find out how matters stood. Frost rejoined his family at Bethlehem to await the settlement. By March 22 he was able to write Sidney Cox, who was now teaching in Schenectady, the Frosts wouldn't be in the poorhouse for five years or so. The $800 a year he had been getting from his grandfather's estate would be continued, and the principal would hold out for just about five years. To his grandson Grandfather Frost had seemed an old-line Democrat with a devil-take-the-hindmost philosophy, but through his thrift he became an unwitting patron of genius. He could not have imagined when he offered his grandson one year to work at poetry that later generations of poetry lovers would call his named blessed for the legacy of financial support he wrote into his will.

Chapter 12

Interlude at Franconia

Once again Frost's neighbors didn't quite know what to make of him. He had been a puzzle to his grandfather and the older generation at Lawrence. At Derry he had been regarded as odd because he had adjusted the milking schedule to his literary hours. At Dymock, in England, some yokels had suspected he was a German. And now in the little village of Franconia, in the long shadows cast by the White Mountains of New Hampshire, they wondered about him because he was unaccountably famous.

He had followed his family back to Bethlehem, and the Lynches with whom they had spent their August before sailing to England. John Lynch was an old Irish patriot who had lost money in Ireland and hated the English, but he and his wife liked the whole Frost family and welcomed their return.

Carrying out their shipboard resolution, Robert and Elinor had looked for a farm to buy. There wasn't much for sale, but they finally found a little farm two miles west of Franconia. It was a real mountain farm on the side of Sugar Hill. From it there was a view of the impressive Franconia range with Mt. Lafayette rising well over 5,000 feet. This view was probably the farm's biggest "sales point" to Robert Frost. Nearby flowed the Pemigewasset River. It had taken a bit of doing to acquire this farm because the owner, William Herbert, had to be persuaded to move off and buy a red farmhouse for himself down the road "a small piece," as they say in New England. Frost tells about this transaction in his satirical poem, "New Hampshire."

> I caught the owner outdoors by himself
> Raking up after winter, and I said,
> 'I'm going to put you off this farm: I want it.'
> 'Where are you going to put me? In the road?'
> 'I'm going to put you on the farm next to it.'
> 'Why won't the farm next to it do for you?'
> 'I like this better.' It was really better.

Herbert had agreed to sell for $1,000, no down payment, but before the sale was closed, gossip told him that Frost was a poet and a poet was "a somebody." He showed up at the Lynches and talked over the sale some more. Wouldn't Frost pay an extra $100? Frost agreed and took possession soon after he had made his first visit to a college.

Visiting colleges to give readings of his poetry Frost calls "barding around." Tufts College at Medford, Massachusetts, started him "barding around," on May 5, 1915. There he first read three unpublished poems that would become everybody's favorites. "Birches," "The Road Not Taken," and "The Sound of the Trees."

Many visitors came to Franconia to see Frost. Such poets as Louis and Jean Starr Untermeyer. Such Professors as Cornelius P. Weygandt, Harold G. Rugg, Joseph Warren Beach.

There was, furthermore, a small colony of writers in the vicinity: a novelist, Ernest Poole, was practically next door to Frost; and a poet, Raymond Holden, was not far away. And there were many telephone calls—from Frost's publisher in New York, from colleges who wanted Frost to read, from hostesses who wanted to capture the new literary lion. But Frost had no telephone. People rang up Herbert who lived "a small piece down the road," and Herbert relayed the messages to Frost and got tired of it.

"Next time you sell a farm, son," said William Herbert's father, "find out beforehand if it's going to be used as a farm or a park."

One day a rural neighbor decided that he would really find out what manner of business this new Franconia farmer was engaged in. He called on Frost on the pretext of selling him seeds. As soon as he got inside, however, he came to the real point.

"How are the books coming on, Mr. Frost?" he asked knowingly.

By then Holt had brought out an American edition of *A Boy's Will* as well as the American edition of *North of Boston.* "Poetry exclusively I believe it is with you."

Frost "allowed" that it was.

"What do you ask apiece for them?" the caller asked very respectfully.

"Seventy-five cents for one and one dollar and twenty-five cents for the other book."

On sure ground now, the visitor informed Frost in a superior manner: "Poole gets one dollar and fifty cents!"—referring to the price of Poole's novel, *The Harbor.*

Little did the visitor know that Frost's books were in demand. Shortly before this nosey neighbor's call, Alfred Harcourt had forwarded to Frost a telegram Holt had received from Christy Matthewson, then regarded as the best pitcher in the two major leagues. The great baseball hero had ordered by wire an advance copy of *North of Boston*. "That was supposed to overwhelm me and it did," was Frost's comment.

Five printings of *North of Boston* were needed in the first year of American publication. Such magazines as the *Atlantic Monthly*, which had rejected Frost in the years before his British success, now besought him for new poems. The *Atlantic* went further in atonement for past neglect and published a critical eulogy of Frost's poetry by Edward Garnett, influential British critic. William Dean Howells, who was thought of as the Dean of American Letters, followed Garnett's eulogy with one of his own in *Harper's*—"here is the old poetry as young as ever." Bates College, at Lewiston, Maine, coaxed Frost to read poems there in May, 1916, and in June he was Phi Beta Kappa poet at Harvard's Commencement.

A signal honor was his election to the National Institute of Arts and Letters, a body of 250 men of letters and artists from whom is selected the American Academy of Arts and Letters. Long afterward it came out that an elderly poet and ambassador, Robert Underwood Johnson had opposed strongly Frost's election, citing Frost's early rejections by magazines as the ground of his case. But such conservative critics as Irving Babbitt and Paul Elmer More, assisted by Wilbur Cross, editor of the *Yale Review*, recognized the humanistic temper and classical quality of Frost's books and overcame the opposition to his election to the Institute.

It was most fitting, too, that Robert Frost should have a connection with a new magazine, *The Seven Arts,* launched late in 1916. *The Seven Arts* heralded the coming revival in American literature. It announced the forces that were to make the 1920's a remarkable literary period. Frost served on its Board of Advisory Editors and contributed "The Bonfire" and the only one-act play he has published, "A Way Out" to its early issues.

The crowning event of 1916, however, was the publication by Holt of his third volume of poetry, *Mountain Interval,* the volume that contains "The Road Not Taken," "Birches," "Brown's Descent," "The Hill Wife," and other poems that have come nearer to being household poems than any others since the days of John Greenleaf Whittier and Henry Wadsworth Longfellow.

There was no doubt now that Frost's success in America would not only continue but would greatly exceed the success of his debut in England.

Chapter 13

Amherst and Michigan

Looking back at the year 1917, Frost has called it "a bad year" for him, despite his growing acceptance as an American poet. In 1917 America entered World War I and the prospects for American poets darkened for a while. In 1917 the war took the life of Frost's best friend, Edward Thomas. On Easter Monday, April 9, only three days after America declared war against Germany, Thomas was killed at Vimy Ridge, near Arras, in the British spring offensive. "He was the bravest and best and dearest man you and I have ever known," Frost sadly wrote to his widow. The depth of feeling Frost had for the British poet produced "Not to Keep," and the poem of lament, "To E.T."

Robert Frost was living in the college town of Amherst, Massachusetts, when he heard the news of Thomas's death. Back when the war was only a few months old he had written Sidney Cox from England: "I should awfully like a quiet job in a small college where I should be allowed to teach something a little new on the technique of writing and where I should have some honor for what I suppose myself to have done in poetry." He had added, "Well, but I mustn't dream." This dream, however, had become fact. He was now an *ad interim* professor of English at Amherst College, and he was finding that teaching three courses was seriously cutting down on his time for composing poetry. In fact, he published only three poems in magazines during the whole year—and this slowing-up of his poetic production gave him another reason for calling 1917 "a bad year."

Frost's appointment to Amherst had resulted from a visit there on December 16, 1916; 40 years of teaching engagements in colleges were to stem from it. Amherst had a remarkable president in Alexander Meiklejohn, a progressive educator, and a remarkable professor of English in Stark Young, later to become a powerful dramatic critic in New York. These two, knowing of Frost's "barding around," invited him to read his poems at Amherst on a cold, mid-December afternoon.

A small audience greeted Frost, who was nervous. But he noticed a man in the front row; there was something he liked about the way this man listened. Frost said "The Death of the Hired Man," and this man came up afterwards to tell him that he especially valued this poem because his own father had been a hired farmhand. Thus began the long friendship of W. R. Brown, Amherst real estate man, with Robert Frost, Amherst professor.

President Meiklejohn was no man to let an impulse cool off, and he immediately made Frost a proposition. Would Frost accept an appointment to the Amherst faculty for the term that began after Christmas? It did not matter, Meiklejohn said, that Frost had no degrees; no, it didn't matter that he hadn't been hewing out an academic career. Defying normal procedure, Meiklejohn was ready to make him a full professor right away. He could, however, pay him only $1,500. Well, Frost wanted to know, could he bard around once in a while? Meikle-john agreed to that, and Frost told his wife when he returned to Franconia, "Just one term. We can stand that."

He had said something like that when he had agreed to teach at Plymouth State Normal School, and he had stayed there just one year. But his "one term" at Amherst was extended to three years before he took a 20-month leave from college teaching.

Early in January the families on "faculty row" saw an old, battered automobile stop before a modest vacant house and saw descend a band of Yankee vagabonds—a poet and his wife, a bevy of youngsters, animals, and even chickens in coops. The Frosts had come down from the White Mountains to the little region in Massachusetts from Northampton to South Had-ley that seemed to have something in its soil that favored the growth of colleges. At Northampton there was Smith College; at Amherst there were Massachusetts Agricultural College and Amherst College; at South Hadley there was Mount Holyoke College—all within a radius of ten miles. And Amherst town had been the home of an earlier New England poet, Emily Dickinson. Robert Frost was happily located.

The following week he was telling his students: "What we do in college is to get over our little-mindedness. Education—to get it you have to hang around till you catch on."

The boys knew that their teacher was refreshingly original when he told them at the outset that "I'll never correct a paper for style. I'm looking for subject matter, substance in your-selves." Frost went to the heart of things.

Amherst students soon discovered that they were on their own with the new professor. They were expected to be their own masters and to go about their own education. The students liked his sense of humor, his playfulness, even when it was hard to know how to take it. Frost never flunked anyone, but he had a challenging way of expecting the student to think for himself. That explains why his courses were never considered "snap" courses.

Sometimes he startled a class by asking at the beginning of the hour: "Why do we have classes anyway?" They learned that he preferred talks with students at his home to classes on the campus. "We were glad to go to his house at ten or eleven at night," one of them remembers, "and sit somewhat uneasily in his sitting room until he came in from some depth of the dwelling and sprawled out on a lounge. He read from this poet and that, throwing the book aside when he reached what seemed to him the furthest reach of luminous expression in some particular poem. And then he would say what occurred to him in relation to that poem, going from there to the general characteristics of poetry."

Frost was something new in college circles, but just what nobody could say.

The way Frost went at things in the classroom made Frost's courses at Amherst unconventional. He was not good at planning an hour with a class. On the way to class he thought of something that would serve as a central thought, and he got himself and his students to talk at random about the subject. Often, before the hour ended, this discussion had taken on a firm shape. An advance had been made in understanding, justifying Frost's remark that "there is such a thing as random talk, but it is to be valued as scouting for coinable gold."

He told his students at the outset: "The lack of ideas in

[*114*]

young minds is shocking to me. That's my quarrel with everybody I know. I want you putting two and two together, and I don't care a hoorah for anything else. That's my interest. As long as I stay around the colleges that will be my reason for staying."

Amherst made him a better offer and he stayed there until 1920. The college boys liked him because he expected much of them. It was a foxy method of teaching, as he explained it. "The good teacher," he said, "knows how to get more out of a student by surrounding him with an atmosphere of expectation than by putting the screws on him." He succeeded in being "the sort of teacher who will reverse the whole relationship between student and teacher as it has been, who will encourage the student to make his own trouble without waiting for his teacher to make it for him, who will turn the teacher's claim on the student into the student's claim on the teacher." He put into practice the revolutionary thought that "courses should be a means of introduction, to give the students a claim on me, so that they may come to me at any time, outside of class periods."

He was a challenging teacher. "The business of the teacher is, I presume, to challenge the student's purpose. 'This is life, your career is ahead of you,' he must say. 'Now what are you going to do about it?' I do not mean that the challenge should be made in words. That, I should think, is nearly fruitless. . . . No, what I mean is that his life must say that, his own work must say that."

In the spring of 1921 Frost received an unusual offer. Won't you come out in the fall, the president of the University of Michigan asked, and become something we call a Fellow in the

Creative Arts for the academic year of 1921-1922? We will pay you $5,000 to do what you will be doing in any case—that is, writing poetry. Only we want you to write here on our campus; we want you to be our poet in residence.

Such an offer was naturally appealing to the poet. He called it becoming "Michigan's Idle Fellow," and he accepted it with a will to fraternize with the aspiring literary students on the Michigan campus. "Mr. Frost will do no teaching nor will he be expected to accomplish anything definite unless he has something authentic to say," the Michigan alumni magazine said.

This was the beginning of a revolution in the teaching of writing. Since Frost's appointment as "poet in residence," many colleges have asked other poets and writers to live on their campuses, to perform light or no teaching duties, but to bring students into contact with the creative spirit in literature while writing their own works.

At Michigan—he was an "Idle Fellow" there for two years—Frost talked a great deal at his home or in other informal surroundings with writers for the undergraduate magazines. In these students he looked for "the weakness, the strength, to be swept away, to be carried away, but something more than beer, and games, and so on. I want everybody to be carried away by something. I'd rather it would be beer and games than nothing, I think. I like people who can't help thinking and talking about things to the highest reaches. That of course is the great thing."

Poetry, he told his Michigan students, has always been something like play. He said he had learned that truth in his baseball-playing days. Yes, "literature is a performance in

[*116*]

words." He emphasized the word *performance*.

"Don't write for A's," he told them. "Athletics are more terribly real than anything else in education because they are for keeps, for blood, and that is the way I want you to write. Studies are done just for practice. Write only when you have something to say."

All his life Frost has liked to compare art to athletics. "The nearest thing in college to the arts is not the classroom," he is fond of declaring. "The nearest thing to the arts is the gymnasium and the athletic field."

As at Amherst, so at Michigan the poet excited the students by expecting much from them. He went so far as to require that they instruct him. "Long ago," he told the Michigan alumni magazine, "I gave up the idea of asking my students to tell me what I knew that I might discover if they knew as much as I did. Now in classes I ask questions in the correct sense of the word, for I want them to tell me something new, something I do not know."

After two years at Ann Arbor, Frost returned to Amherst and the teaching of regular courses again—only these were unusual courses. The first was a philosophy course. The professor who had been giving it had died, and Frost had been asked to suggest possible candidates. He had been indulging a great leaning in himself toward philosophy, and he concluded his search for candidates by suggesting himself. He got the job. The other course was on minor writers. "You'll be reading off the main stream," he told the opening class. "Borrow, Cobbett, plays and things."

After the two courses got under way, Frost wrote a friend: "I don't teach. I don't know how. I talk and have the boys talk.

[*117*]

This year I'm going to have two courses, one in literature and one in philosophy. That's funny. I don't know that I know much about either. That's the reason perhaps that we get along so well. In the course in literature we're going to read a book a week. They're not going to be major authors, the classics of literature, either. They're going to be minor writers—people that aren't so well known. Why do I do that? For a reason that I think rather good. Those boys will, in the course of their education, get the first rank people whether I include them or not. That's what education very largely means today—knowning the names that sound the loudest. That's what business means, that's what success means. Well, I'd like to get out of that rut for a while. I'd like to get the boys acquainted with some of the fellows who didn't blow their trumpets so loudly but who nevertheless sounded a beautiful note. We're not going to read the works in class: we couldn't do all of that. The boys will do their reading at home. They'll read in class the things that appeal to them most. An incident. A bit of dramatic action. I'll let them choose what they wish; I'll let them read what they wish. And then we'll have some fun in their telling me why they made their choice, why a thing called to them."

The course was aimed at the enjoyment of literature. "I don't want to analyze authors," Frost said in a most unprofessorial manner. "I want to enjoy them, to know them. I want the boys in the classes to enjoy their books because of what's in them. . . . Youth, I believe, should not analyze its enjoyments. It should live."

Unconventional as he was, still Frost gave grades—but never a failing grade. "I have never complained of having had to mark," he said. "I had rather mark anyone for anything—for his looks, his carriage, his ideas, his exactness, anything you please—I would rather give him a mark in terms of letters, A, B, C, D, than have to use adjectives on him. We are all being marked by each other all the time, classified, ranked, put in our place, and I see no escape from that. I am no sentimentalist. You have got to mark, first of all, for accuracy, for correctness. But if I am going to give a mark, that is the least part of my marking. The hard part is the part beyond that, the part where the adventure begins."

The final examination Frost gave at the end of his minor writers course in 1923 has become a legend. When the students assembled to take the examination, Frost wrote on the blackboard, "Do something," and left the room. The young reader may well ask himself what he would do, just as those Amherst boys tried to puzzle out what their professor was demanding of them. It was indeed a poser.

Some of the boys thought that Frost was expressing his contempt for the examination system and that he meant for them to leave at once and "do something" at the fraternity house. This was in line with their inclination toward pastimes. Others thought that he meant them to come to his office and say good-bye. They climbed the stairs to his office, knocked, and told him that they felt they had gotten a great deal from his course. But from his manner they could not tell if they were passing the "do something" examination. Others—and they were quite unimaginative—crammed into the blue examination books everything they could recall that Frost had said during the course. Only a couple sat and thought about their personal discoveries during the course. One wrote a thoughtful paragraph; the other recounted an incident that embodied a memorable philosophical discovery. With these Frost had succeeded. They "did something" on this unique examination.

Stimulating though Frost was to his students, he himself was restless at his Amherst post and chafed against the set ways of the institution. In 1925 he packed his household goods and returned to Ann Arbor—for good, he thought. For the University of Michigan had not only renewed the Fellowship in Creative Arts, calling it now a Fellowship in Letters; but it had raised the pay to $6,000, an important consideration since Frost's children, even though adult, were still dependent. Furthermore, this appointment was part of the regular budget of the University and was for an indefinite period, not a year-to-year arrangement as it had been the first time he had gone to Ann Arbor. And so Frost moved back to Ann Arbor, with every expectation that he who had been born in the Far West, and lived in New England for four decades, would become a Midwesterner the rest of his life.

At Michigan he tried to make his student gatherings into something like the old Greek symposiums. "It is the essence of symposiums I'm after," he declared. "Heaps of ideas and the subject matter of books purely incidental. Rooms full of students who want to talk and talk and spill out ideas, and suggest things to me I never thought of."

Chapter 14

"Barding Around"

A fter two years Frost pulled up the roots he was putting down in Ann Arbor and came back to Amherst once more. He was even willing to take a reduction in pay to teach at Amherst, for the job there was tailored for him and promised to give him considerable time for himself. "You're a tramp," the prominent Amherst trustee, Dwight Morrow, had told Frost. "Well, we are creating a job for you in which you can tramp around." Frost would have plenty of time to "bard around" at other colleges and plenty of time for writing poetry in solitude.

In that fall of 1926, he "barded" at Wesleyan University for two weeks, staying in the home of his friend, Wilbert Snow, Maine coast poet and English professor. One of Snow's students, a 20-year-old junior from New Hampshire, Lawrance Thompson, paid rapt attention to every word Frost uttered. Thompson listened intently the night Frost explained that "the freedom I'd like to give is the freedom I'd like to have. That is much harder than anything else in the world to get—it's the freedom of my material. You might define a school boy as one who could recite to you, if you started him talking, everything he read last night, in the order in which he read it. . . . That's just the opposite of what I mean by a free person. The person who has the freedom of his material is the person who puts two and two together, and the two and two are anywhere out of space and time, and brought together. One little thing mentioned, perhaps, reminds him of something he couldn't have thought of for twenty years." Thus began Thompson's con-

As a teacher, Frost had plenty of time to "bard around."

centration on Frost that ultimately produced an excellent critical study of Frost's poetry, *Fire and Ice*. Later on Thompson traveled about with Frost, making notes and collecting material for an authorized biography of the hero of his undergraduate days at Wesleyan.

About this time Robert Frost began to "bard around" at the annual Bread Loaf Writers Conferences that Middlebury College started in the Green Mountains of Vermont. He had been a co-founder of the Bread Loaf School of English in 1920 and had been an annual lecturer there ever since. But the writers conference idea was something else and something new. It was to be unacademic; it was to bring together professional writers and editors and aspiring young writers for two weeks of individual and group conferences; and it was to fill in the time at the Bread Loaf Inn between the mid-August closing of the summer School of English and Labor Day, the traditional closing date for mountain inns. Frost was a sort of godfather to the early Bread Loaf Writers Conferences; later he became the great central figure at them, even though he spent most of the time offstage. The Bread Loaf conferences started a new movement in adult education, and today there are some 40 writers conferences held each summer.

Frost knows how to make an audience laugh. At Bread Loaf and elsewhere he is fond of telling about the student whom he commanded to produce so many pounds of manuscript before he passed him.

"There was one fellow—I don't know where he is now, but he became a professor. I started talking to him about using his own judgment. The most terrible thing is your own judgment. He set out suffering. I never saw the writing at all. He let me think he was suffering agonies. Never wrote anything.

"One day I said to him, 'Bill,' I said, 'you haven't written anything, have you?' He said, 'No, sir.' I said, 'Now, look, we've done this on the high too long. You want to graduate?' He said, 'Yes, sir.' I said, 'Now we're goin' to do it on the low.

I'm not going to *read* what you write. But you're going to deliver to me so many pounds of it to weigh.'

"One night he came over to me in the library, where I was sitting with a student, and produced another pound. "I had put him through a lot of agony, so he deserved to graduate."

On one occasion a member of the Bread Loaf conference asked Frost about his interest in baseball.

"The latest book I bought," Frost told the writers assembled, "is an encyclopedia of the World Series. You know what I was looking for in it? When I was away, out of the country, the World Series was won by the Boston Braves, in 1914. One of the pitchers was a boy I knew, Lefty Tyler. The Braves came up from the bottom. He is only mentioned once in the encyclopedia, but there were three pitchers that day, one for the other side and two for the Braves. One of them was James; the other was Lefty Tyler. Whether he pulled James out of it, or James pulled him, I don't know. My hero. I am always interested in games." (James pulled Tyler out.)

Another question from the Bread Loaf group was: "Which of your poems do you like best?"

"Ask a mother which of her children she likes best. She won't tell you. I have no favorite poems, and if I had, I wouldn't tell you. I want to be fair to my poems."

In 1931, still "barding around" from Amherst, Frost gave a ten-lecture course at the New School for Social Research in New York. This was the first of many engagements he was to keep at the New School. The method of his first course, the school catalogue announced, would be "one of soundings for meanings, rather than one of general analysis."

[*124*]

Although Frost refused to allow a stenographic recording of his New School lectures, a number of his statements were copied down verbatim and subsequently published in a magazine in England.

At the beginning, Frost said that "writing is a measured amount of what you could say if you would—if you wanted to," and this, for all its colloquialism, is as classical as the famous definition of literature as "speech considered at leisure." Frost was uncompromising about this. "Only just as much as we can communicate is literature," he told his New School audience. He made a brilliant try at defining form: "Form is a balance expected, missed and compensated for."

Frost had much to say about tone of voice. "First idiom, and then vocal images." "Tones exist, and we collect them." "The audible page." "Our sentiments and our tones of voice are very close together." "Sound is more important than the visual, because closer to sentiment."

Again he quipped: "The terms extravert and introvert are just legpulling by metaphor. I nearly extravert when I hear these terms. I'm just a vert from the country."

In his concluding talk he gave a fine definition of creation: "Creation has its end implicit in the beginning but not foreknown." Finally, he said that "everything depends on where the poem rises. If the source is pure, the poem will be. The source and the flow is all there is to it. Purity of source and purity of mood. A critic is a person who can tell right off the source of a poem."

Always he returned from his "barding around" to his home base at Amherst where he was Professor of English on the John Woodruff Simpson Foundation and where he had happy relations with such colleagues as Professor George F. Whicher and Professor G. R. Elliott. Elliott had written an interesting essay, "The Neighborliness of R. F.," in which he had noted that Frost wrote "the poetry of true neighborliness" and expressed the "persistent spirit of patient, laborious neighborliness." This, Elliott said, was different from "the romance of human brotherhood," "the wider ideal of human brotherhood." This distinction between "the facts of human nature in the immediate neighborhood" and the sentimental dream of brotherhood are important to understanding Frost's social views.

"Barding around" from a home base went on for 12 years until Frost abruptly cut his ties to Amherst in 1938.

Chapter 15

"At Present I Am Living in Vermont"

I n the fall of 1920 Robert Frost and his family had moved from New Hampshire—"a most restful state," he said—to Vermont and he became for the next 40 years what he called "a vert from Vermont." It was an important move. Frost gave the impression that it was a sudden and impulsive move. He had liked Franconia in the White Mountains very much. It was good for his hay fever during his annual time of suffering, and he was to return to Franconia during the hay fever season several times after he had left the state. Still he had grown restless at Franconia, and one morning in September 1920 he piled his family into his old automobile and by night they were arranging their belongings in "an entrancing stone house" they had admired in South Shaftsbury, Vermont. That is the way Frost tells it—they just up and moved like that.

But the move to the white-clapboarded, green-shuttered town of South Shaftsbury had been carefully planned. They had looked at at least three houses with longing, speculative eyes before choosing and buying the old Peleg Cole house that stood on the Peleg Cole hilltop. This old stone house, built about 1783, was indeed entrancing to a New Englander. It was described by a neighbor—Dorothy Canfield Fisher, the writer, who lived at Arlington only ten miles away, that in old Vermont being only a neighborly distance—as "homelike and strong and cheerful and protecting . . . standing wide-roofed and substantial, with its old lilac and syringa bushes, and the lily-of-the-valley bed." There was a real barn across the way and there was an orchard of fruitful apple trees. From his direct and indirect earnings as a poet, the poet had acquired a fine house, a good barn, and a real farm.

At first the whole Frost family—Robert, Elinor, Leslie, Irma, Carol and Marjorie—lived happily in the old Peleg Cole house on the hill. In a couple of years Carol married a Vermont girl and she joined the family in the old stone house. In another two years Robert and Elinor moved out and gave the house to Carol and his wife, who raised apples and sweet peas for a living. The older Frosts took another house in South Shaftsbury, called The Gulley, and occupied this until 1938, the most dreadful year in Frost's life.

Frost was now a Vermonter for good. Summers from 1928 onward, he would drop in at the Bread Loaf Writers Conference on a mountain about ten miles from the campus of Middlebury College. Here he would say his poems, take part in a round table discussion, give an informal talk—and play tennis.

After supper on a June night in 1922 in the old stone house at South Shaftsbury, Robert Frost sat down to write a long poem. He had been thinking about this poem for some time. He had a pretty good notion of what he wanted to say

[*128*]

because, before leaving Michigan for Vermont, he had given a talk to a Chamber of Commerce group of men. He remembered the ideas in this talk; now he must feel them as poetry. The poem started easily.

> *I met a lady from the South who said*
> *(You won't believe she said it, but she said it):*
> *'None of my family ever worked, or had*
> *A thing to sell.'*

He always liked to say that a poem should begin in delight, and this one did. His pen moved easily on.

> *I don't suppose the work*
> *Much matters. You may work for all of me.*
> *I've seen the time I've had to work myself.*

He was starting a poem that would be quite unlike any poem he had yet written. The time had come to make it plain that he was an individual poet making his personal discoveries and proceeding on his own way. He was no member of a group. He had a fine reputation in America, but there had been a mistake in the recognition given him. Too often he had been mixed into a new wave of writers, too often it had been assumed that he was part of a new movement in American literature that was to dominate the 1920's.

In truth, Frost was apart from, not a part of, the new literary currents. Free verse was the vogue and he did not free-versify. Romanticism and revolt were the mood, and he was classical and traditional by temperament. He didn't like the free verse of Carl Sandburg with his love of the blur, his dreamy

[*129*]

laziness, his drifting impressionism. There was free-versifying Amy Lowell, shallow and decorative. She wanted Frost to write in dialect, stupidly said he had no sense of humor, thought he depicted a decadent, morbid New England. There was Edgar Lee Masters and his best-selling, free-verse *Spoon River Anthology,* a complaining, disillusioned man. There was Vachel Lindsay—well, Frost rather liked him; still Lindsay was various things—sentimental, picturesque, declamatory—that Frost was not. It was time to correct the impression that he belonged in attitude and spirit and aim to the so-called "new poetry." To correct it, he chose to write a satire, and that was the business of this June night in Vermont in 1922.

More than the other poets of his generation Frost loved the Latin poets, Virgil and Horace. Indeed, it is tempting to call him the Yankee Virgil. There are superficial resemblances. Both came of yeoman stock. In their youth, both "failed" at everything but poetry. Both, after a good start in making poems, studied philosophy. Both were late in publishing their first books, and both had great success. Both retired to farms. But all this is superficial. The more important connection is between the pastoral poetry—the eclogues which Virgil wrote, and the eclogues which Frost put into his second book, *North of Boston.*

Frost liked the satire that Horace, a contemporary of Virgil, wrote as much as he enjoyed Virgil's eclogues. Horace was another farmer-poet. Horace liked to write rambling compositions in verse, a sort of poetic medley, that criticized the follies of men. Horace did this in the form of good-natured and friendly conversations with himself and others. He made easy, casual use of anecdotes and symbols and often ended a satire

[*130*]

with a light jest. Frost was attempting a Horatian satire as
darkness fell. He did not foresee the miracle that would
come at dawn. He happily rounded off the first stanza.

> *The having anything to sell is what*
> *Is the disgrace in man or state or nation.*

The first target, then, was the folly of commercialism.
Then the poet thought of a traveler from Arkansas who
boasted that his state had commercial quantities of diamonds
and apples—of a Californian who boasted that nobody died
a natural death in the wonderful climate of California—of
a bibulous poet who was "selling" the idea of protesting in
verse against Prohibition—he thought of these and said:

> *It never could have happened in New Hampshire.*

He had come upon the theme and title of his poem.

> *Just specimens is all New Hampshire has,*
> *One each of everything as in a show-case*
> *Which naturally she doesn't care to sell.*

As midnight came on, he described the specimens. The
newly-rich man who came back from California and built a
pretentious mansion in the New Hampshire woods. One President of the United States: Franklin Peirce ("pronounce him
Purse," the poet wrote). One Daniel Webster. One family descended from pre-Indians. One unnamed reformer.

Did you but know of him, New Hampshire has
One real reformer who would change the world
So it would be accepted by two classes,
Artists the minute they set up as artists,
Before, that is, they are themselves accepted,
And boys the minute they get out of college.
I can't help thinking those are tests to go by.

One guess. Right. The "reformer" is Frost himself. Just the sort of humorous allusion to himself Horace often made.

The list of specimens continued. A chicken fancier from Philadelphia. A tiny gold mine: "Just enough gold to make the engagement rings/And marriage rings of those who owned the farm." One old-style witch. This led the poet to digress from New Hampshire to a new-style witch he met at a cut-glass dinner in Boston, but soon he is back to a vigilante committee in New Hampshire.

Now came another Horatian touch, a digression to tell about buying his farmhouse in Franconia.

The night was getting on, and Frost was still writing.

Apples? New Hampshire has them, but unsprayed.

He was off again for more fun.

A state producing precious metals, stones,
And—writing; none of these except perhaps
The precious literature in quantity
Or quality to worry the producer
About disposing of it. Do you know,
Considering the market, there are more

Poems produced than any other thing?
No wonder poets sometimes have to seem
So much more business-like than business men.
Their wares are so much harder to get rid of.

Well did he know how hard it was to get rid of poems to editor-buyers. He had earned a meagre total of $200 dollars in his first 20 years of making poems.

It was time, he now reflected, to include Vermont in the poem. After all, he had moved there two years ago. New Hampshire, he wrote, was one of the two best states in the Union. *"Vermont's the other."* He smiled as he thought of the absurdly small towns in each state. Especially Still Corners. This tiny place was so named not because it was so quiet nor because it had a whiskey still; but because it hadn't grown. It was "still corners" and not the city it dreamed of being.

It was a funny thing about the loud laugh that the big place laughed at the little place. His pen raced along.

New York (five million) laughs at Manchester,
Manchester (sixty or seventy thousand) laughs
At Littleton (four thousand), Littleton
Laughs at Franconia (seven hundred), and
Franconia laughs, I fear,—did laugh that night—
At Easton. . . .

which had cast six votes in the 1912 presidential election.

Anything I can say about New Hampshire
Will serve almost as well about Vermont,
Excepting that they differ in their mountains.

[*133*]

But some poets had belittled New Hampshire men and women. Amy Lowell, for instance. She couldn't stand them; had said to him: *"Read your own books and find out"* what's wrong with them. Now was the chance to reply to that; now he could set the record straight.

> *I may as well confess myself the author*
> *Of several books against the world in general.*

Don't you see, he seemed to be saying, that I am a conservative who is opposing the general trend of the age throughout the world in general? I am not writing just about man in New Hampshire; my criticism of life—if that is what it is—is universal, and applies to all mankind.

As for friends in New Hampshire: *"I thought they couldn't be* [better than those I left behind in Massachusetts]. *And yet they were."* And the people have a *"foundation of well-being."* You could call them lucky and comfortable.

> *For art's sake one could almost wish them worse*
> *Rather than better. How are we to write*
> *The Russian novel in America*
> *As long as life goes so unterribly?*

Some of them reach a high level of intelligence. Like a Warren farmer who defined the trouble with the Mid-Victorians as being caused by Darwinism, and another farmer who burned down his farmhouse to buy a telescope because he was curious about the stars.

Time for a jest. Instead of worrying about elevating the people, why not plan to elevate New Hampshire's already lofty mountains. This thought was good for nearly fifty lines of play-fulness.

It was toward dawn now. The climax was reached.

Lately in converse with a New York alec
About the new school of the pseudo-phallic,
I found myself in a close corner where
I had to make an almost funny choice.
'Choose you which you will be—a prude, or puke,
Mewling and puking in the public arms.'

Frost's first answer to that was:
'Me for the hills where I don't have to choose.'

But he was cornered by the New York smart-alec. Man-fully he explained that he wouldn't be a prude afraid of nature.
"I'd hate to be a runaway from nature."

But neither would he be one of those self-expressers, a writer who throws reticence to the winds and pours out his private life to the public ear.

And neither would I choose to be a puke
Who cares not what he does in company. . . .

At last—was the clock striking four?—he offered us the key to his whole poetic philosophy.

How about being a good Greek, for instance?

It was characteristic of Frost that he should shape his key like a question-mark, but his meaning was unmistakable. He was writing books against the world in general because he was trying to be a good Greek in New England. It was this aspira-tion, this classicism of spirit, that set him apart from the "New

[*135*]

Poetry" movement that flourished from 1914 to about 1925.
Like Horace, Frost ended his satire with a light jest.

I choose to be a plain New Hampshire farmer
With an income in cash of say a thousand
(From say a publisher in New York City).

"Whose woods these are I think I know."

It's restful to arrive at a decision,
And restful just to think about New Hampshire.
At present I am living in Vermont.

This had been quite a night's writing. True, he had prepared for this feat. And the form of "New Hampshire" was casual, relaxed, loose. Thus he was able to write out the poem fluently and rapidly. "I rattled it off at home—fact," he said, and then hedged just a little: "I almost did that." Possibly he worked on and revised the first draft for some time afterwards.

Dawn was at the poet's window as he wrote the last line. He rose, went out into the early light for a few minutes, then came indoors again.

And then a miracle came to pass. A poem suddenly "just came" to him. He crossed the room and wrote it down "in one stroke of the pen," one of the finest lyrics in English.

Stopping by Woods on a Snowy Evening

Whose woods these are I think I know.
His house is in the village though;
He will not see me stopping here
To watch his woods fill up with snow.

My little horse must think it queer
To stop without a farmhouse near
Between the woods and frozen lake
The darkest evening of the year.

He gives his harness bells a shake
To ask if there is some mistake.
The only other sound's the sweep
Of easy wind and downy flake.

The woods are lovely, dark and deep,
But I have promises to keep,
And miles to go before I sleep,
And miles to go before I sleep.

Chapter 16

A Weekend with Frost

B oth of the poems Frost wrote on that happy June night in 1922 went into the book he published in 1923, his first book in seven years. The long poem became the title poem of the new book, *New Hampshire*.

The following year the Pulitzer Prize for poetry was awarded to Robert Frost for *New Hampshire*. Although the Pulitzer Prizes had existed for only a few years, a Pulitzer award was already a high honor. He was to win it again in 1931, 1937, and 1943, by which time the prize had gained in prestige until it was the highest American award a poet could win. No other poet has been a four-time winner.

Academic honors also began to be bestowed on Robert Frost in 1924. Middlebury College and Yale University gave him the honorary degrees of Litt. D. (Doctor of Letters), and ultimately he was to receive more than 40 such honorary degrees from colleges and universities. As each degree means the receipt of a multi-colored silk hood, the poet has been faced by an unusual wardrobe problem: what to do with such an accumulation of academic finery. *"It's knowing what to do with things that counts,"* he says, quoting a line from one of his San

Francisco poems, and what he did with the 40-odd hoods was to have them cut up into squares and pieced together to make elegant coverings for a pair of quilts. This disposition of the silk hoods is certainly one that our great grandmothers, if they were of New England stock, would have thought of.

Most writers are not subjects of biographies until it is clear that their work will outlast their lives. Now and then, however, the critics and the public agree during the lifetime of the writer that his work has permanence, and because of that, a biography of him while he is still in his prime is wanted. This was clearly the case with Robert Frost; and early in 1927, when Frost was only 52, a biography was commissioned. I was the writer commissioned to write a short, critical biography of this poet I had come to admire very much. One day in February of 1927 I took the train for Amherst, Massachusetts, to spend several days with the "good Greek" I took Frost to be.

The man who came onto the porch of his rented house as I alighted from a taxicab struck a quiet but vivid note. He was a large man with a big-boned, rugged frame. Poised on the strong neck was a large, finely modelled head that gave a lyrical accent to the countryman's body. There was an elfin quality about his eyes and mouth. The countenance of the man welcoming me was immediately winning with its sensitivity, its fluent gravity, and its friendly lines. There was a trace of shyness in his manner; at the same time there was ease in its simplicity.

Inside the house I was greeted by Mrs. Frost, quiet, sweet, intelligent, and devoted. Talk began and in a little while dinner was served. I was in for three days of the best talk of our time, for Robert Frost is a great talker as well as a great teacher and a great poet. He carries on the great tradition of literary table talk, and it is the world's gain that such friends as Sidney Cox and Reginald L. Cook have remembered his sayings and collected them in books about him.

At dinner Frost asked me many questions about New York literary life. It was soon evident that he kept pretty much out of it, nor did he follow the current literary reviews and books with steady attention. Yet he had his own way of keeping up with literary doings—a countryman's way. He pumped persons who came from the metropolis and he got his news from their lips, not from print. So on this evening he asked me about *The Dial,* the monthly magazine of the arts that all the young writers were striving to appear in, and I remember that he asked about William Carlos Williams, the New Jersey poet and novelist.

After coffee, we settled down comfortably in the living room for a long session of questions-and-answers about his life. Frost talked and ruminated, told stories, made critical observations, and speculated. I was especially fascinated by the note of speculation in his talk, for this meant that his mind and his emotions had growing ends. He was curious and alive as if he were a youth.

He talked at length that night about his Indian-fighting ancestor, Major Charles Frost. The Indians had hated him, and after they had finally killed him from ambush on July 4, 1697, they had desecrated his grave. They dug up the body, carried it to the top of Frost's hill, and suspended it from a stake. The Indians, it seems, had a long memory back to an incident that had occurred at Dover, New Hampshire, in 1676 near the close of King Philip's War. The Indians were supposed to

[*141*]

have had a friendly conference with the white men, but the white men played a trick on them—for which the Indians blamed Captain (as he was then) Frost—and seized 400 of the red men.

For years, Frost told me, he had looked on this ancestor with some disapproval. He considered him the black sheep in the family whom other people honored for his treacherous conduct at the Indian conference. But lately he had learned that Major Frost had objected to the treacherous stratagem and had entered into it with great reluctance.

"I am glad to think a little better of the old settler," Frost said.

Then Frost drifted into reminiscence of San Francisco days and his father's tragic life. There was something deep between Frost and his father. The father was mentally alert. He was ambitious, as his political activity revealed. And, despite his illness, he was strenuous. Once he engaged in a six-day walking race with the champion, Dan O'Leary. He won, too. O'Leary, Robert Frost told me, had sworn that he could give Frost's father a liberal handicap and then walk him down. When O'Leary failed to do so, he claimed that Frost's father had violated the rules of walking. Afterwards O'Leary and the elder Frost became friends. But the really deep bond between father and son seems to have been a sense of tragedy in one's view of the world. His father's character excites a kind of awesome regard in Robert.

Then the talk shifted to the London scene . . . to the fooleries of a forgotten free verse poet named Skipwith Cannell and Ezra Pound . . . the jiu jitsu demonstration Pound made on Frost's person in a restaurant . . . the time Pound and Frost were invited to luncheon by two ladies, and Pound was disgusted by their shallow flow of talk on art; he rose, knocking his chair over as he did so, and said to Frost haughtily, "I leave these ladies to you."

It was past two in the morning by then. The family was mentioned. Carol and Irma were married. Lesley had been running a book shop in Pittsfield, Massachusetts, but she was planning to go around the world and manage a bookstall on the ocean liner. Marjorie, who wrote poetry, had not been well for some time.

Finally, Frost remarked: "A poem is an idea dawning. If you have it before you write it, it will be like translating it into poetry; but if you feel it as it is making in your mind, then it is a poem. If it hasn't that freshness of dawn on it, it isn't a good poem."

The college clock struck three, Frost's usual bedtime. I went to my room to write down all I could remember of his talk. Tomorrow he would be up around eleven, a student or two would call with some writing for him to read, and at one o'clock we were to be driven to a farm house for "a real New England luncheon," and later there would be a walk.

On the next evening Frost talked fondly of his friends in publishing. Alfred Harcourt at Henry Holt's. Harcourt had left Holt to found his own publishing company, and Frost had been tempted to follow him. But he had liked the man who had taken Harcourt's place at Holt's, a sensitive, intelligent man named Lincoln MacVeagh, and he had stayed put. Then MacVeagh had left to run a new publishing house, the Dial Press. What should he do now, Frost wondered, about a publisher? Well, that problem wouldn't come up for a while.

He didn't have a new book ready.

Then he spoke of an Amherst professor he admired. "He loves the classics and he is a *field* scientist." There were scientists Frost didn't like. He expressed his doubts of the "bunko-sciences," which it appeared were mostly sociological and psychological.

He spoke next of a night spent with Paul Elmer More, the literary critic, at Princeton. Then he told one of Padraic Colum's Irish stories.

I was glad when he got on the subject of his friendship with Thomas Bird Mosher, the printer of beautiful editions of the blue china poetry of the 1890's. Mosher had quite early picked one of Frost's poems out of affection and printed it in his catalog. Poor Mosher! He had gone into a sad decline. He was an epicure, and of all things to happen to an epicure, he had lost his sense of taste. In desperation Mosher had beefsteaks specially sent from Boston to Portland and specially prepared by the best cooks he could engage, only to find them tasteless to him. But his fine literary taste was still unimpaired.

He chatted a while about J. J. Lankes whose woodcuts had illustrated his most recent book, *New Hampshire.* Frost had admired the feeling for New England landscape Lankes had revealed in some woodcuts reproduced in the *Masses* and the *Liberator,* radical magazines of eight or ten years earlier. And Lankes had admired Frost's poetry and had illustrated several of the poems for his own private enjoyment. Then poet and woodcut artist were brought together by Carl Van Doren, an editor of *The Century,* in a fortunate collaboration for which each, unknown to the other, had already been prepared.

Somehow the talk shifted again. Nature, Frost explained,

[*144*]

does not complete things. She is chaotic. Man must finish her tasks, and he does so by making a garden and building a wall. That garden is art.

"One of the real American poets of yesterday," Frost went on to say, "was Longfellow. I am not being sarcastic. I mean it. It is the fashion nowadays to make fun of him. I come across this pose and attitude with people I meet socially, with men and women I meet in the classrooms of colleges. They laugh at his gentleness, at his lack of worldliness, at his detachment from the world and the meaning thereof. When and where has it been written that a poet must be a club-swinging warrior, a teller of barroom tales, a participant of unspeakable experiences? I hear people speak of men who are writing today, and their eyes light up with a deep glow of satisfaction when they can mention some putrid bit of gossip about them. 'He writes such lovely things,' they say, and in the next breath add, half worshipfully, 'He leads such a terrible life.' I can't see it. I can't see that a man must needs have his feet plowing through unhealthy mud to appreciate more fully the glowing splendor of the clouds. Inspiration doesn't lie in the mud; it lies in the clean and wholesome life of the ordinary man. I am an ordinary man, I guess. That what's the trouble with me. I like my school and I like my farm and I like my people. Just ordinary, you see."

"An extraordinary ordinary man," I murmured to myself as I made notes on that evening's conversation.

An "Original 'Ordinary Man' " his old friend Sidney Cox called Frost in a long essay published by Holt a couple of years after Frost had told me that "I like the middle way, as I like to talk to the man who walks the middle way with me."

[145]

Chapter 17

"How About Being a Good Greek?"

I 1928 Robert Frost's fifth book, *West-Running Brook,* was published. The title came from a brook on his Derry farm so named because the other brooks in the vicinity ran east.

In that year Robert and Elinor, accompanied by their youngest daughter Marjorie, revisited England. They saw the surviving friends of their stay in England from 1912 to 1915—Helen Thomas, widow of Edward Thomas; Wilfred Gibson; W. H. Davies, a hobo turned poet. "You still interested in poetry, Frost?" Davies asked jocularly. "I'll give you a book with my autograph."

The Frosts crossed over to Ireland and there encountered a friend from America, the poet Padraic Colum, who was visiting his native land. Colum showed Frost about Dublin. But let Colum tell this in his own words.

"We were in Dublin, Robert Frost and I. As the car swung into a courtyard, 'Where are we now?' he asked. 'In Dublin Castle.' 'What does one do in Dublin Castle?' 'If one is an American,' I said, 'one goes into that office and asks for a genealogy.' It was the office of the Ulster King-at-Arms. 'I'll do it,' Robert said. 'What name, sir?' asked the genealogical expert. 'Frost.' 'Lincolnshire Frosts or Somerset Frosts?' Robert did not know. 'What Christian name is usual in the family?' 'Robert,' 'Lincolnshire Frosts. There are tombstones. . . .' He named the places. 'Then I want the genealogy of the Lincolnshire Frosts. . . . Will you tell me what arms I get?' 'A grey squirrel and a pine tree, sir.' "

From England the Frosts went on to Paris and lived quietly on its outskirts for a while. They liked England but were not cosmopolitan enough by nature to wax enthusiastic about France, as so many Americans do.

Back home, Frost wrote a poem, "The Lovely Shall Be Choosers," which he added to *West-Running Brook*. The book was already published, and he could not add it at once, but in his *Collected Poems* a year or so later, he inserted "The Lovely Shall Be Choosers" in the "West-Running Brook" section. It is the only poem in free verse that Frost has published. He has always been an opponent of free verse, but in this poem he shows that his opposition was not based on lack of skill in *vers libre*. What he was opposed to was "lazy verse," which some people contended was all that free verse was. An even more interesting fact about "The Lovely Shall Be Choosers" is that it is about Frost's mother, Belle Moodie Frost. He imagines how she looked in her youth:

> But she stood straight still,
> In broad round ear-rings, gold and jet with pearls
> And broad round suchlike brooch,
> Her cheeks high colored,
> Proud and the pride of friends.

He recalls how his mother had once told him and his sister

Jeanie about the brightness of her youth:

> *Give her a child at either knee for fourth joy*
> *To tell once and once only, for them never to for-*
>   *get,*
> *How once she walked in brightness,*
> *And make them see it in the winter firelight.*

In 1929 came the first Robert Frost–Spiral Press Christmas card. A young man in New York, Joseph Blumenthal, had entered book publishing and become enamoured of fine printing and beautiful editions. He left publishing for printing, mastered the art, and set up his own Spiral Press. He soon made a reputation for exquisite taste.

As Christmas 1929 approached, young Blumenthal cast about for a subject for his personal Christmas card. He thought of Frost's poem, "Christmas Trees," which bears the subtitle, "A Christmas Circular Letter." Would that not make a wonderful Christmas card? In fact, that was what it had been back in 1915. Frost had sent out a homemade card that year on which in his own hand he had written this poem about a man who wanted to buy a thousand Christmas trees at three cents apiece and was sent away empty-handed. So Blumenthal hand-set the type for "Christmas Trees" and printed cards for himself and his wife and certain members of the Henry Holt publishing firm. That was the beginning of an annual custom in which Frost has collaborated. Each year since 1929 a poem has been chosen, artwork has been prepared, Blumenthal's "crisp, severe, venturesome" taste has selected the paper and type and governed the printing—and hundreds of friends of the Frosts and the publisher have said: "This is the most beautiful

[*149*]

of the Christmas cards I have ever received."

The Frosts came to have many, many friends—from the younger years when he was a teacher and made such lifelong friends as John Bartlett and Sidney Cox. Now at the height of his career there were hundreds of friends—students, professors, writers, men in government, men in various walks of life like W. R. Brown, the Amherst real estate man, John W. Haines, the British lawyer who had tramped the Gloucestershire countryside with him, and Richard Thornton, editor at Henry Holt's. Collectors, too, were appreciators of these Christmas cards, for by now Frost items were fetching good prices in the rare book and manuscript market.

In 1930 Robert Frost received the high honor of being elected to the American Academy of Arts and Letters. The Academy is a section of the National Institute of Arts and Letters of which Frost had become a member in 1916. Membership in the Academy is limited to 50 who are chosen from the 250 members of the National Institute.

Such an honor was all very well, but Frost values the making of poems above all honors; and it is therefore likely that the big event for him in 1930 was the appearance of his *Collected Poems*. He had had five books published—*A Boy's Will* in 1913, *North of Boston* in 1914, *Mountain Interval* in 1916, *New Hampshire* in 1923, and *West-Running Brook* in 1928. The critics spoke of his permanence. He was 56. It seemed to his publisher the right time to declare that Frost was a major American poet who would outlive his period and be read by posterity, and it was so declared by publishing the *Collected Poems*.

The year 1930 could be called a breathing spell in the creative life of Robert Frost. His *Collected Poems* seemed to put a period to his production of poetry. Nobody thought that he was finished. But nobody dreamed that more than thirty years of making poems still lay before him. The volume of his work was respectably large. Anyway, poets were supposed to slow down after the prime of life. To the readers of 1930 it seemed unlikely that there would be more than a slender book or two of poems to add to the *Collected Poems*. As time would unfold, however, Frost would publish at least six more books and bring out an edition of the complete poems besides. But those readers of 1930 felt, when the *Collected Poems* came into their hands, that the time had come to place Frost in the history of American poetry.

What sort of poet was he anyway? Had he really been writing books against the world in general? What did he mean about being a good Greek in New England? These questions came to the fore as a decade of great change began. In the midst of change Frost seemed to be standing still on an eminence, a high eminence, of poetic achievement, but just what had his achievement been?

Frost may have been standing still in that fateful year when America reeled from the shock of the economic crash of 1929-30, but the literary scene around him exploded into a full-scale "battle of the books." In 1930 began the heated controversy over the New Humanism. Two writers of the older generation, Irving Babbitt and Paul Elmer More, had been developing a doctrine of life and letters that took the name New Humanism. This doctrine had been expressed by Emerson in his lines about the human law and the law for things.

> *There are two laws discrete*
> *Not reconciled—*
> *Law for man, and law for thing;*
> *The last builds town and fleet,*
> *But it runs wild,*
> *And doth the man unking.*

The doctrine drawn from these lines is called dualism. Dualism is a twofold view of man and the world. The dualist sees man as made of two elements—a human element and a natural element—spirit and matter. This dualistic doctrine of two laws, one for man and one for thing, had attracted a number of followers, mostly in the universities, who were, as one might say, spoiling for an argument with the leaders of American literature in the 1920s. The New Humanists said that this had been a decade of revolt. They called the leaders of the revolt Romantics and charged that they followed the law for things.

Masters and disciples finally joined in a symposium, *Humanism and America,* to challenge the revolt and disorder of the times. An uproar from literary journalists greeted this book and a big controversy ensued for a year and a half.

Robert Frost was not enlisted on either side in this "battle of the books." He has never been a man to wear a label of any kind, nor does he take part in the strife of critics. He shuns rigid systems, and he thought the New Humanism was rigid. He lets his poems speak directly to the reader for themselves, and he never explains them. Nevertheless, although he stood apart from the argument between the New Humanists and the

Romantics, his position in American poetry was put in a strong light by the battle-flares both sides sent up. In this strong light it could be seen what kind of poet Frost was. He could not be called a New Humanist, yet he was certainly a poet that Babbitt and More and G. R. Elliott, the Amherst Humanist critic, approved of. In their eyes Frost was a poet of humanistic temper.

To begin with, Robert Frost was really deeply versed in country things. He knew very well the line between Man and Nature. He had botanized on many a long walk, and at night he had studied the heavens. His humanistic—indeed, his classical temper—was revealed in his well-known poem, "On the Need of Being Versed in Country Things." This poem tells about a farmhouse that had burned down and the barn that was falling to pieces. The birds came through the barn's broken windows and nested inside. The poem concludes:

> *For them there was really nothing sad.*
> *But though they rejoiced in the nest they kept,*
> *One had to be versed in country things*
> *Not to believe the phoebes wept.*

Now a romantic poet, writing about sighing over the ruins of human habitations, would have ended this poem with what is known as a pathetic fallacy. The romantic poets would certainly have had the phoebes weeping over the sad fate of the house and barn.

But Frost never indulges in the pathetic fallacy. He has accepted a dualistic world of Man and Nature. He has expressed contentment with his lot of joy and love "dashed with pain and weariness and fault." In his poetry Nature is a friendly antagonist, dangerously strong, but on the whole a fair opponent. Thus, in "The Need of Being Versed in Country Things" he accepts nature as lovely and fair, but he is aware of its unconcern for man's disasters. The birds have taken possession of the old place and the lilac renews its leaf for them and so does the aged elm, but Nature grieves not for man. To be versed in country things is to observe distinctions, and Frost's sense of demarcation between Man and Nature is clearly classical.

He is classical, too, in his handling of rhyme and meter and verse-forms. Not for him "the new ways to be new" of experimental poets. He teased them and stuck unfashionably to "the old ways to be new."

Frost was like an intelligent Greek, the New Humanists said, because he was, as they put it, of a positive and critical turn of mind. His classical outlook was evolved in a simplified world, the world of the New England farmer from about 1885 to about 1915. This farmer had a settled routine of living according to the seasons of the year. He led a village life in which he thought he knew most of the human elements at work—could see and touch them and measure them. In those years the intricacies of commerce and industry, the distress wrought by the machines, the flow of vast crowds, the diversity of appeals of a great city, did not reach him. That was to come later, as was the great shift of population from rural to urban areas. Churches were what they had been, intellectual currents did not disturb, and science, arch-upsetter of former values, was only a rumor. Toward science at large the attitude was indifference. In Frost's New England many of the complex and tormenting questions that have arisen since the small city and farm communities of old Greece had not entered into the problem of living in the horse-and-buggy era. *"Me for the hills where I don't have to choose,"* Frost said in 1923 when invited to face the dilemmas of modern life.

The people Frost wrote about lived in a tamed wilderness and were disciplined by it. In New Hampshire, Frost said, the mountains were not high enough. Nature was not extravagant nor unduly wild, nor were the people of Frost's poems grandiose or expansive. They had bodies that were hardened by toil. Their emotions were rock-like. And their minds had a lot of good sense. These New Englanders had a settled social framework—or so it seemed at the time. Their struggle for existence was an honest one, and they gained a fair amount of well-being. Nature did not allow them to be lazy or to cheat but she gave fair returns to honest struggle.

Frost's rule in writing about these people was the one he had advocated to John Bartlett and his other students at Pinkerton Academy: "Common in experience—uncommon in writing." "Common in experience"—that meant that Frost was an observer of two laws of humanistic art: the law of probability and the law of decorum or measure or proportion. He was the poet of the common in man and nature, not the exploiter of the unique and wonderful. And he had a feeling for decorous proportion—another classical trait. Frost achieved permanence in his art by teaching himself the golden mean of the Greeks.

The best appraisal of Frost's place in American poetry was made in 1936 by Mark Van Doren, himself a poet, in an essay entitled "The Permanence of Robert Frost."

"Mr. Frost's place is and always has been singularly central," declared Van Doren, "His range has been great enough to carry him close to all the corners, yet he has never quite

[155]

crossed a line. He has always, in a kind of silence and with a most remarkable integrity, kept to his center." Van Doren points out that Frost's centrality is not a consequence of compromise. Frost doesn't avoid extremes or compromise between them. Frost's way "consists in occupying or touching both extremes at once, and inhabiting all the space between." At one extreme Frost has written a religious poem, "The Trial by Existence." At the other he has written a naturalistic poem, "Out, Out—," that could well have been an incident in a raw, violent novel: a buzz saw severs the hand of a boy who dies from the shock. All the space between raw naturalism and religious insight has been occupied by Frost, and this space may properly be called the humanistic space. Finally, Frost's way, Van Doren said, "consists in finding that golden mean which, far from signifying that the extremes have been avoided, signifies that they have been enclosed and contained."

Chapter 18

"Let Eliot Read One and I'll Write One"

On the evening of November 16, 1932, Robert Frost dressed for dinner and went to Boston's famous St. Botolph Club. In another part of the city, T. S. Eliot also dressed for dinner and headed for the St. Botolph. The two men were to meet each other for the first time.

Early in the 1920's, Eliot, now a rival for the honor of being America's premier poet, had come to notice. Fourteen years younger than Frost, he overcome this handicap with a single long poem of disillusionment, *The Waste Land,* which made a great stir. Rapidly his influence spread in England, where he lived after graduation from Harvard, and in America, where he had been born in St. Louis, Missouri. Eliot became the leader of the modern movement in poetry, and his followers regarded Frost as a traditional poet. By 1932 in the estimation of many the modern Eliot had displaced traditional Frost and had become first poet of our land.

Frost was not happy as he entered the club. Long afterwards he admitted that he was jealous of Tom Eliot, who had come from England to give a course of lectures at Harvard. "I began the evening a bit antipathetic," Frost has confessed. "A touch of the old jealousy and suspicion that Eliot had replaced me in the not too good graces of Ezra Pound. The jealousy that I felt after Eliot's poetry began to appear, and after Pound's efforts for him began to bear fruit."

Frost's jealousy was not petty; there was nothing small about his rivalry with Eliot. Frost, in the language of sport, is an intense competitor. He plays poetry to win. For 20 years he had been mostly denied publication while lesser poets pushed into print all around him. Then at last he had been discovered and received his due. And now, so soon after his triumphs, he appeared to be slipping from the high place he had won, and a new tendency in poetry was becoming fashionable. All this aroused the competitor in him, just as a veteran baseball star will compete against the brilliant rookie who is out for his job.

Young champions of Frost were seated at the dinner table: handsome Robert Hillyer, lyric poet, already nursing a dislike of Eliot's poetry that would explode years later in a furious attack on the man; and Theodore Morrison, teacher at Harvard, the new director of the Bread Loaf Writers Conference, and a poet too. Morrison and his wife, Kathleen, were already started on one of the longest and closest of the many friendships Frost was to win. Glancing around the table, Frost saw David McCord, composer of delightful light verse; John Brooks Wheelwright, an eccentric poet, very, very Bostonian; and Ferris Greenslet, editor at the old publishing house of Houghton Mifflin, and chief arranger of this dinner in Eliot's honor. At the head of the table sat the host, Robert G. Dodge, the president of the St. Botolph Club. At his right was the tall, slender, fine-featured T. S. Eliot. Frost himself sat next to John Livingston Lowes, the small, wiry Harvard professor who had made a sensation in literary circles with his book *The Road to Xanadu,* about the imaginative process of the poet Coleridge. In all there were about 25 guests, a group of the elite in Boston's cultural life.

A tension was noticeable as the first course was served, and there was expectation of a clash of the two rivals. The expectation was finally fulfilled late in the evening. Eliot, a critic of high standards as well as a poet of great distinction, remarked that Robert Burns could not be considered a poet at all. This assertion was heretical enough, but Eliot went on to say that no poetry had been written in Scotland since William Dunbar, who had lived from 1465 to about 1520. This was too much for the Scotch Frost had inherited from his mother.

"Eliot sounds like a Border name," said Frost, referring to the wild country lying along the boundary between England and Scotland, the scene of battles between Scots and English and between river Border lords.

"We were Somerset Eliots," T. S. Eliot replied, naming the county in southwest England.

"Might we consider Burns a song writer?" Frost asked with ironical emphasis.

"One might grant that modest claim," the judicious Eliot conceded.

This little passage between the two poets was reported in the newspapers in a heightened form. According to the papers, Robert Frost had risen from a sickbed to defend Burns at the St. Botolph dinner. The truth was that Frost came down with the flu after his defence of Burns.

Earlier in the evening there had been a humorous incident. As the guests smoked their cigars after coffee, Mr. Dodge, the host, read two early poems by Eliot: "The Boston Evening Transcript" and "The Hippopotamus." It seemed to the guests that Eliot was slightly uncomfortable at the choice—he had grown religious since he had written these secular poems—and someone proposed that both Eliot and Frost read a recent poem of their own.

"I will if Frost will," Eliot said with his usual courtliness of manner.

But Frost demurred.

"I'm sorry. My *Collected Poems* has just recently been published and I'm ready to loaf."

General disappointment was, of course, expressed all around the table. Frost saw that he would have to yield. Very well, he would give play to his Puckish self.

"Let Eliot read one and I'll write one."

He borrowed place cards and concentrated on writing stanzas on their backs. At last he was ready. Eliot read a recent poem and Frost "said" what was presumably his most recent poem:

A Record Stride

In a Vermont bedroom closet
With a door of two broad boards
And for back wall a crumbling old chimney
(And that's what their toes are towards),

I have a pair of shoes standing,
Old rivals of sagging leather,
Who once kept surpassing each other,
But now live even together.

They listen for me in the bedroom
To ask me a thing or two
About who is too old to go walking
With too much stress on the who.

I wet one last year at Montauk
For a hat I had to save.
The other I wet at the Cliff House
In an extra-vagant wave.

Two entirely different grandchildren
Got me into my double adventure.
But when they grow up and can read this
I hope they won't take it for censure.

I touch my tongue to the shoes now
And unless my sense is at fault,
On one I can taste Atlantic,
On the other Pacific, salt.

One foot in each great ocean
Is a record stride or stretch.
The authentic shoes it was made in
I should sell for what they would fetch.

But instead I proudly devote them
To my museum and muse;
So the thick-skins needn't act thin-skinned
About being past-active shoes.

And I ask all to try to forgive me
For being as over-elated
As if I had measured the country
And got the United States stated.

It is not likely that Eliot believed that this skilfully fashioned poem was impromptu. Nor has any of the guests at this memorable dinner ever stated that he believed Frost wrote "A Record Stride" on the spur of the moment when he said: "Let Eliot read one and I'll write one."

What everyone was sure of was that the Puck in Frost put on "a good act."

Chapter 19

"A World Torn Loose"

In 1930 Robert Frost had entered upon the unhappiest decade of his life.

Nobody liked the Great Depression which deepened from the stock market crash of 1929 to the temporary closing of the banks in 1933 when Franklin Roosevelt was sworn in as President. In that short time industry slowed down and the number of the jobless rose to the unheard-of figure of at least 10,000,-000. Soup kitchens multiplied and bread lines lengthened. America had never known such hard times. Farmers lost their farms. Businesses went bankrupt—31,000 failures in 1932—and big banks failed. Out-of-work men sold apples on the streets. An economic blight lay over the land, and did not spare Frost's region, New England.

Frost watched the rural world that he had loved go into a steep decline. A gradual decline in New England agriculture had begun long before. New England had by the time of the Great Depression become citified to a large extent and industrialized. Now the decline here was sharp, too. In the early 1930's such New England smoky mill towns as Lawrence, where Frost had grown up, seemed to be dying. Society was changing before Frost's eyes and he did not like the new urban ways. He was versed in country things and scornful of the "smart alecs" in the cities.

To counteract the forces of the Depression, President Roosevelt called for a New Deal, a set of measures designed to promote the welfare of the stricken nation. These measures were enacted by Congress, and the government set up agencies to perform public works, provide jobs, and revive the economy.

Robert Frost viewed the New Deal with a country cousin's suspicion. That is putting it too mildly. He was very hostile to it. His wife, a Republican, was even more hostile. It was hard for the friends of Robert and Elinor Frost to understand their deep antagonism to the new social measures. For several years it seemed that Robert Frost could talk of nothing but the sins and stupidities, according to him, of the New Dealers.

Frost is not sentimental about people. He is not a humanitarian. This does not mean, however, that he was callous about people's sufferings in the hard times of the 1930's. He was not a humanitarian, as his friend G. R. Elliott had showed, but he was and is a friendly and neighborly man. He was too much of an individualist to support the New Deal. He was too skeptical of its methods to believe the New Deal would achieve its ends. In the heat of the controversy over the New Deal, one poet called Frost a counter-revolutionary poet. "You're a bargain-counter-revolutionary poet," Frost wittily retorted. The New Deal philosophers, Frost felt, offered to set too low a price on democracy. He himself remained a sturdy democrat, and protested that the New Deal was not good for democracy.

Frost was also disturbed by the literary criticism he received in the dark decade of the 1930's. He had been overlooked and largely unpublished in the first 20 years of his writing life. In the next 15 or 20 years he had been welcomed and almost overwhelmed with recognition of his stature as a poet like Frost who wrote about a democratic rural life was an critics had been praiseful. But, as the country slid deeper into economic depression, detractors of Frost's poetry appeared. Some of these, like the poet who dubbed Frost a counter-revolutionary, had political motives for crying down his poems. One effect of the Great Depression was the movement of many writers to the Left. They placed great hope in Soviet Russia. They were impressed by the theory of communism. They praised the literature of the working-class or proletariat, as they preferred to say. To these Leftist writers, an individualistic poet like Frost who wrote about a democratic rural life was an out-of-date fellow, a literary back number who stood against the revolutionary times. History, they muttered, would take care of relics like him.

History, however, was quite soon to take care of Frost's political detractors. Events in Russia disillusioned them. The Hitler-Stalin pact in 1939 was a bombshell that scattered them. Most of the writers on the Left speedily repented and came back to the center of literary America.

Just as numerous as the detractors were the patronizers of Frost. The advance guard of poets and readers were following the leadership of T. S. Eliot and Ezra Pound, expatriates who lived in London. Eliot had stayed there and become a British subject. Pound had moved to Paris in the mid-1920's and subsequently had gone on to Rapallo, Italy. To the devotees of "modern" poetry, Frost was a sort of second-class citizen of the Republic of Letters, and they spoke patronizingly of his traditional rural poetry. It hurt Frost that Ezra Pound, who had been the original backer of his poetry, had become the chief supporter of Eliot's *The Waste Land*—had, in fact, given editorial advice that Eliot had gratefully acknowledged.

Why is Robert so disturbed by the detraction and patronizing he is receiving? his friends wondered. His place in American literature is secure. Why should he feel that other poets are threats to his security? What they did not understand was how deeply Frost had been hurt by the 20 years of neglect from graduation day at Lawrence High School in 1892 to Ezra Pound's discovery of him in 1912. He had been accepted at last, but there remained the fear that he would be eclipsed and neglected again. Was the period of his acceptance and esteem to be a short one, only 15 years or so, and was he to be thrust aside by new poets and new tastes? He never doubted the worth of his poetry, but he was tormented with doubts of the stability of the poetry-reading public. He was afraid of a shift in taste that would leave him stranded.

Long after his bad decade of the 1930's Robert Frost wrote a poem, "One Step Backward Taken," that stated how he felt in the years that led up to the outbreak of World War II in 1939.

> *Not only sands and gravels*
> *Were once more on their travels,*
> *But gulping muddy gallons*
> *Great boulders off their balance*
> *Bumped heads together dully*
> *And started down the gully.*
> *Whole capes caked off in slices.*

I felt my standpoint shaken
In the universal crisis.
But with one step backward taken
I saved myself from going.
A world torn loose went by me.
Then the rain stopped and the blowing
And the sun came out to dry me.

But the sun did not come out until the later 1940's.

Frost took "one step backward" to sanity whenever he wrote a poem in the 1930's, and he wrote three of his best in that period. In 1932 he travelled to California—the first time he returned to his native state—and there wrote his poem about the people keeping watch on the beach: "Neither Out Far Nor In Deep"—one of his most profound poems. In 1935 he composed his satire on university bureaucracy, "Departmental," which at once became a favorite of the poet's public readings. In that same year he wrote "The Gift Outright," which critic after critic has called our best patriotic poem and which an audience of millions heard the poet recite on Inauguration Day in 1961.

In 1936 his sixth book, not counting the *Collected Poems* of 1930, was published. He called it *A Further Range* because he was extending his subject matter beyond New England. His themes now became less regional and more national in scope. The universal note deepened in his work. The dedication of *A Further Range* was to the poet's wife and reveals his intention of broadening the range of his poetry from the regional to the national and even the global.

"To E. F.," the dedication ran, "for what it may mean to

her that beyond the White Mountains [New Hampshire] were the Green [Mountains in Vermont]; beyond both were the Rockies, the Sierras, and, in thought, the Andes and the Himalayas—range beyond range even into the realm of government and religion."

Despite the detractors and the patronizers, there was no let-up in the honors accorded to Frost. In 1931 he received for the second time the Pulitzer Prize for poetry. He was a professor on very liberal arrangements at Amherst until 1938. He gave the celebrated Charles Eliot Norton Lectures at Harvard in 1936.

The titles of his six Harvard lectures tell us much about his poetic creed. They were: I. The Old Way to Be New; II. Vocal Imagination, the Merger of Form and Content; III. Does Wisdom Signify?; IV. Poetry As Prowess (Feat of Words); V. Before the Beginning of a Poem; VI. After the End of a Poem. He talked to overflow crowds. Said the *Boston Evening Transcript:* "They were standing all the way up and down the side aisles, sitting on the window ledges, standing in the balcony at the back, sitting on the floor in the center aisles, and on the platform steps and along its edge. By a quarter past seven most of the seats were taken, and by half past none were left." Frost began to speak at eight. This popularity was reassuring in the midst of the drift of poets and readers to the banners of Eliot and Pound.

In 1937 Frost received the Pulitzer Prize for the third time. In 1938 he received a singular honor. The governing body of Harvard University is a Board of Overseers. Although Robert Frost was a non-graduate of Harvard, he was persuaded to run for overseer. By a larger alumni vote than any Harvard

[*168*]

alumnus ever received, non-graduate Frost was elected to the Board.

In that same year Richard Thornton, Frost's friend at Henry Holt, collected a number of writings about Frost and put them into a handsome volume, which he entitled *Recognition of Robert Frost*. In 1939, to complete this catalog of honors, a second *Collected Poems* was brought out by Frost's publisher; and soon after its appearance, he was awarded the Gold Medal for Poetry by the National Institute of Arts and Letters.

These honors were only a lining of the dark clouds of personal trouble, sorrow, and tragic grief that all but crushed the poet by 1940. He had been troubled at the outset of the decade by the break-up of the marriage of one of his daughters. Then he had been stricken by the death of his youngest daughter, Marjorie, who had been threatened with tuberculosis but had recovered enough to become happily married. Marjorie wrote genuine poetry. After death had taken her, her parents collected her verse in a privately printed volume.

Beginning in the winter of 1934-35, Robert and Elinor Frost went to Florida for the cold months. The first year they stayed in Key West, the next they spent at Coconut Grove. In the winter of 1937-38 they stayed at Gainesville, Florida, and there on March 20, 1938, after 43 years of marriage, Robert Frost lost the wife who had meant so much to him. He had been ill with influenza. She had nursed him. Suddenly she succumbed to a heart attack.

"Elinor Frost," said the poet in his grief, "is now more in my six books than she is anywhere else on earth."

At first the poet felt that he could not live on. He severed his tie with Amherst College and sold his house at Amherst.

His loneliness and desolation were almost unbearable.

Finally, to make his cup of sorrow overflow, his son Carol committed suicide in 1940. Carol had never achieved financial independence on his little farm at South Shaftsbury. He, too, had tried to write poetry but editors had refused it. Knowing of Carol's despondency, Robert Frost had made a special trip to see him and talked a whole night through with him. Two days later Carol shot himself. The report of Carol's gun climaxed the end of the black decade for Frost.

Chapter 20

Years of Renewal

Sometime in 1940 a renewal of the spirit occurred in Robert Frost. He came out of wintry despair and entered a springtime of advancing years.

Perhaps this renewal started with the purchase of the Homer Noble farm at Ripton in the Green Mountains of Vermont. Ripton is about eight miles from Middlebury where Middlebury College was founded in 1800 and about two miles from the Bread Loaf Inn where Middlebury College each summer sponsors the Bread Loaf Writers Conference. Frost had known this hamlet for 20 years. He had been co-founder of the Bread Loaf Summer School of English near Ripton. In 1924 Middlebury College gave him the first Litt. D. he received. A few years later he acted as godfather to the Bread Loaf Writers Conference—and each August he had showed up there to "say" his poems, to talk informally to the students, to take night walks with the faculty.

Frost has a keen eye for real estate and he had long noted the 300-acre Homer Noble farm. It was wild, wooded, and, like so many New England farms, deserted. It stood on a hillside and had many features he had written poems about: brooks

[*171*]

and old cellar holes and farm houses. He looked with appreciation at a log cabin with a big stone fireplace. That would make an ideal shelter from May to November for a widowed poet in his late 60's. He bought the farm and made himself comfortable with his shepherd dog Gillie in the log cabin. He refused to put in a telephone. He didn't need one because down the hill his friends Theodore and Kathleen Morrison moved into a large farmhouse that had a telephone. Unlike Farmer Herbert at Franconia, the Morrisons would gladly take his messages.

Mrs. Morrison—she had been Kathleen Johnston then—had first heard Frost "say" his poetry at Bryn Mawr College in 1920, and she had formed a deep acquaintance with his work in the years that her husband Theodore was directing the Bread Loaf Writers Conference and teaching at Harvard. In 1939 she began to be an unofficial secretary to the poet. He had neglected his business papers after his wife's death. Mrs. Morrison helped him to put them in order, and in time came to handle much of his correspondence, as well as screening visitors who in increasing number came to his cabin porch. She found him an apartment in Boston in 1939, and in 1941 helped to install him in a house he bought at Cambridge. This house wasn't far from the sites of the houses of James Russell Lowell and Henry Wadsworth Longfellow. Always Frost connects with the long American past.

There was plenty of date-arranging for Mrs. Morrison to do, for Frost was again much in demand. From 1939 to 1942 he was Ralph Waldo Emerson Fellow in Poetry at Harvard. In 1943 he went west to Indiana University to be Poet in Residence for a while. Then he became Ticknor Fellow in the Humanities at Dartmouth College. As a freshman he had run away from Dartmouth. He came back as a teacher. He quoted Shakespeare's sonnet: "Let me not to the marriage of true minds" to his students, and added a prose thought: "Science measures height, but can't measure worth. Science will never know."

In 1942 he published his sixth book, *The Witness Tree*. It was a continuation of the further ranges he had explored six years earlier in *A Further Range*. Less and less was he a regional poet in the new book. More and more he was the national poet, the universal poet. *The Witness Tree* contained "The Gift Outright" that President-elect Kennedy invited Frost to read it at his Inauguration. Frost ventured far from New England to write about an incident on a slave ship or to compare a lady to

"a silken tent
At midday when a summer breeze
Has dried the dew"

In one epigram he compressed all his skeptical wisdom:

We dance round in a ring and suppose
But the Secret sits in the middle and knows.

The new book included a fine poem about the American flag —"Not of School Age"—which Frost wrote in 1932 but did not publish until ten years later. That poem ends:

He was too young to go,
Not over four or so.
Well, would I please go to school,
And the big flag they had—you know

The big flag, the red—white—
The big flag, the great sight—

He bet it was out today,
And would I see if he was right?

Frost's patriotism was ardent in World War II. He had modified his former severe opinion of President Roosevelt and now liked his war policy. His hatred of the New Deal weakened, and he even sent a modest campaign contribution to his friend, the poet Wilbert Snow, when Snow ran on the Democratic ticket for lieutenant governor of Connecticut. Snow, who was elected, was an outspoken, enthusiastic Democrat.

It had become a habit. For the fourth time the Pulitzer Prize for Poetry went to Robert Frost, this time for *The Witness Tree.*

Many visitors came to the Ripton summer home. Family visitors, of course, mostly grandchildren, for Carol and Marjorie were gone and daughter Irma had become a chronic invalid. But Lesley would come with her two daughters, and the children of Carol and Marjorie would come, too, to see grandfather, who might now be called *Tête d'armée nouveau* —head of a new army of youngsters. Intimate friends like the George F. Whichers from Amherst stayed on the farm, and for several summers Lawrance Thompson, now a professor at Princeton, came with his growing family. Thompson's *Fire and Ice: The Art and Thought of Robert Frost* was published in 1942. On many evenings a Middlebury College professor would stop at the farm and listen intently to Frost's free-ranging conversation. Afterwards he made notes and meditated on the man and his poems. The fruit was a scholarly book, *The Dimensions of Robert Frost,* by Reginald L. Cook, published in 1958. With Theodore Morrison summering there,

[*174*]

Ripton was a sort of poets' colony and sometimes must have caused Frost to remember that earlier poets' colony at Dymock in England where he had happily written some of his best poems.

He was writing steadily in the 1940's. Three more books were prepared and published: *A Masque of Reason* in 1945; *A Masque of Mercy*, 1947; *Steeple Bush*, 1947.

Steeple Bush contained one of the wisest of Frost's poems: "Choose Something Like a Star." A poem begins in delight, Frost has said, and ends in wisdom. "Choose Something Like a Star" begins playfully. But the poet then asks the star for some word that will serve as a stay against the confusion of life. "I burn," says the star, which is an answer only in terms of man's knowledge, an answer in terms of science. The poet demands more. Finally the poem ends in wisdom.

> *O Star (the fairest one in sight),*
> *We grant your loftiness the right*
> *To some obscurity of cloud—*
> *It will not do to say of night,*
> *Since dark is what brings out your light.*
> *Some mystery becomes the proud.*
> *But to be wholly taciturn*
> *In your reserve is not allowed.*
> *Say something to us we can learn*
> *By heart and when alone repeat.*
> *Say something! And it says, "I burn."*
> *But say with what degree of heat.*
> *Talk Fahrenheit, talk Centigrade.*
> *Use language we can comprehend.*

Tell us what elements you blend.
It gives us strangely little aid,
But does tell something in the end.
And steadfast as Keats' Eremite.
Not even stooping from its sphere,
It asks a little of us here.
It asks of us a certain height,
So when at times the mob is swayed
To carry praise or blame too far,
We may choose something like a star
To stay our minds on and be staid.

Frost's two masques are entertaining, and much more. The characters in the first, *A Masque of Reason*, are Job, Job's sharp-tongued wife, God, and Satan. The time is Judgment Day. The action constitutes the 43rd chapter of the Book of Job in the Bible. There are only 42 chapters in the Book of Job, so Frost has dared to write the 43rd. In this continuation of the Bibical story, God tells Job that there is no connection a man can reason out between his just deserts and what he gets. This He had demonstrated in his treatment of Job. Man must learn his submission to unreason. Moreover, God says that He was showing off to the Devil when He counted on Job's loyalty.

In *A Masque of Mercy* the scene is a bookstore in a large city. The chief character is Jonas Dove (or Jonah, famous for his sojourn in the whale's belly), Keeper (short for My Brother's Keeper), Paul (the apostle), and Jesse Bel (Keeper's wife). The argument is about God's injustice and how it is only bearable if "mercy-crossed." *"Nothing can make injustice just but mercy,"* says Keeper in the last line of the masque.

One more sign that this was a decade of renewal is the fact that Frost's long breach with Amherst College ended. In 1948 Frost was given the degree of Litt. D. by Amherst, and in 1949 he was appointed Simpson Lecturer in Literature at Amherst where he had begun his college teaching back in 1917.

The decade of renewal closed with the publication of the big volume of *Complete Poems of Robert Frost*. All his ten books were in its 642 pages. Here were more than 300 poems he cared to preserve. Pointing to the book, the poet said proudly to his biographer, Elizabeth Shepley Sergeant: "There I rest my case."

> *And were an epitaph to be my story*
> *I'd have a short one for my own.*
> *I would have written of me on my stone:*
> *I had a lover's quarrel with the world.*

Chapter 21

Symbol of America

O n July 10, 1956, nearly 30,000 fans at Washington, D.C., watched the American League All Stars play the National League. Among them was the ageless poet.

"I never feel more at home in America than at a ball game."

[*179*]

He had been given a very good seat because the magazine *Sports Illustrated* had asked him to write his impression of the game. "The All-Star Game is an All-American affair," the editors reasoned in print. "Therefore, appropriately *Sports Illustrated* invites America's greatest living poet to sit in the grandstand as guest columnist."

In the first inning, a photographer snapped Robert Frost as he closely watched Johnny Temple of the Cincinnati Redlegs lead off at bat. In the second half of the first, Harvey Kuenn of the Detroit Tigers came to bat. This was a nervous moment for Frost, for he was rooting for the Nationals. The photographer snapped a picture of Frost rubbing his brow. Cra—ack! Kuenn's bat smashed a sinking line drive in the hole. Impossible for Ken Boyer of the Cardinals to catch it. But he did. He dove far to his left, speared the ball, fell hard to the ground, and hung on to the ball. Frost relaxed and grinned broadly, and the alert photographer caught that, too.

Frost told his readers a week hence that "I never feel more at home in America than at a ball game be it in park or sandlot."

Robert Frost had become a beloved national figure. He had grown into a symbol of America. Frost is American in his devotion to baseball. He has played the game and has bodily memories of the experience. He felt it in his muscles, he said, when Boyer at third base made the two impossible catches, for Boyer in the fifth inning was to rob Kuenn of another hit. Frost remembered as he wrote about the All-Stars that he had been a relief pitcher in games at Bread Loaf but that had been soft ball games, which "I despise like a picture window." He had been proud of his friendships with big league pitchers. He had known Lefty Tyler of the old Boston Braves and Ed Lewis, the National League pitcher who became a college president.

And he had always insisted, as he did again in his *Sports Illustrated* piece, that "the nearest of kin to the artists in college where we all become bachelors of arts are their fellow performers in baseball, football and tennis." Yes, college athletics are "close to the soul of culture."

In a fooling mood he had once promised that he would write a poem about Babe Ruth—the Sultan of Swat—who belted a ball so hard that it never came back but went into orbit around the earth. He had even thought of the opening lines:

It was nothing to nothing at the end of the tenth
And the prospects good it would last to the nth.

Baseball was in Frost's muscles, in his heart, and in his mind on that tenth of July when his team, the Nationals, beat the American All-Stars 7-3. "Perfect Day—A Day of Prowess," he headed his impressions. "Prowess of course comes first," he wrote, "the ability to perform with success in games, in the arts and, come right down to it, in battle." These sports-and-arts sentiments of Frost are the sentiments of America.

This growth of Frost as a representative American, as a symbol of America, took place all through the 1950's. It had started on March 24, 1950, when the U. S. Senate did an unprecedented thing. It passed a resolution of felicitations at Robert Frost on his supposedly approaching 75th birthday. (Frost reached his 80th birthday in 1954, for he discovered while reading through old family letters that his birthyear was not 1875, as he had always supposed, but 1874.)

The Senate resolution struck the keynote of the next decade in Frost's life. It cited his poems for having "helped guide American thought with humor, and wisdom, setting forth to our minds a reliable representation of ourselves and of all men." The framers of this resolution had found a pretty good way of saying that Frost was a symbol of America.

Frost's later emergence as an international figure representing America was thus spontaneous and unforced. It would not be correct to say, as some did, that Frost became a sort of poet laureate—an official poet—for the United States. A poet laureate is expected to write poems to order for national occasions, and Frost is no man to write on assigned themes. Some people who objected to calling him America's Poet Laureate called him America's Bard. Both felt they were borne out when President Kennedy invited him to say a poem at the Inauguration. But President Kennedy chose him because he felt, along with millions at home and millions abroad, that Robert Frost was somehow a symbol of America.

Frost, the people felt, is what an American should be. He is as American as an eagle and apple pie and baseball and Concord, Massachusetts, where "the shot heard round the world" was fired, and where Emerson lived. His speech is Yankee. He is national in spirit and has a firm faith in democracy. His life went straight back to Emerson's New England in which he had grown up, back to San Francisco in which he had been born, back to Revolutionary War ancestors. The four greatest Americans, Frost said, were Washington, Jefferson, Lincoln, and Emerson. Perhaps, his admirers said, the name of Frost would some day stand with Emerson's as a representative American.

[*182*]

His popularity grew as the decade of the 1950's lengthened. His books sold like best-sellers. Perhaps his sales will catch up to Longfellow, our most popular poet, whose sales have reached several million.

Two months after the U. S. Senate honored Frost on his birthday in 1950, the American Academy of Arts and Letters honored him by inviting him to deliver the Blashfield Address at its annual New York meeting. The "address" Frost gave was a long whimsical poem, "How Hard It Is to Keep from Being King When It's in You and in the Situation"—a poem which showed that there was no slackening of his powers with the advancing years. Indeed, by the end of the decade there were enough uncollected poems by the now ageless poet to make a new volume of verse, *In the Clearing*, his eleventh book if we do not count the collected and complete editions. His continued production of poems has rendered *The Complete Poems of Robert Frost* of 1949 incomplete.

One of the new poems went back to his boyhood days.

Auspex

Once in a California Sierra
I was swooped down upon when I was small
And measured but not taken after all
By a great eagle bird in all his terror.

Such auspices are very hard to read.
My parents when I ran to them averred
I'd been rejected by the royal bird
As one who would not make a Ganymede.

[*183*]

> *Not find a barkeep unto Jove in me?*
> *I have remained resentful to this day*
> *When any but myself presumed to say*
> *That there was anything I couldn't be.*

Was there an actual incident like this in Frost's boyhood? During a summer in the Sierra foothills back of Santa Cruz, Rob Frost did go off by himself. He cut through deep woods to see a boy, and returned alone. As he was crossing a bridge, a great eagle swooped down and tried to carry him off. That is what he told his parents. But did this happen? Frost has admitted that in boyhood he liked to tell stories that would raise a sensation. Maybe he invented this tale. He is very unsure whether it ever happened . . . but he has made a fine poem of the fantasy, if that is what his eagle-snatching tale is.

Another new poem characteristically combines humor and wisdom. "The Objection to Being Stepped On" tells how the poet stepped on a hoe, causing the handle to spring up and crack him in the head. It ends:

> *But was there a rule*
> *The weapon should be*
> *Turned into a tool?*
> *And what do we see?*
> *The first tool I step on*
> *Turned into a weapon.*

"One More Brevity" is the finest "dog poem" ever written, and is said to be a sort of elegy for Gillie, the great black-and-white sheep dog who enjoyed for years a special relationship with Frost. Gillie was called Frost's "personal shadow . . . responsive, vigilant, intuitive," and one poet, visiting Frost in his Ripton cabin, declared afterward that Frost "spoke dog" when he made sounds to Gillie. "One More Brevity" is a disguised account of this relationship in which Gillie is replaced by Dalmatian Gus.

Frost's international celebrity become greater than ever. In 1952 he was given a Litt. D. by Durham University at Durham, England. In the same year he was a delegate to a World Congress of Writers at São Paulo, Brazil. In 1954 our State Department sent him to Brazil where he found himself constantly blamed for American materialism. He explained that "ours is a Christian adventure into materialism."

In 1957 he made a trip to the British Isles and collected a garland of honorary degrees. Both Oxford and Cambridge Universities conferred the Litt. D. on Frost. This was the first time these world-famous universities had joined in giving an honorary degree to the same American since they had honored James Russell Lowell and Henry Wadsworth Longfellow. To complete the honors of that summer, the National University of Ireland also gave Frost a Litt. D.

"Are you overtired?" his host at Cambridge asked Frost after this round of degree-acceptance.

"I shall be all right once I get back to Vermont."

He grew comfortable at Ripton in these latter years. He has split up among friends and relatives the 300 acres he bought in 1940. Quite a large Frost clan came to gather up there each summer—six grandchildren and eleven great grandchildren. Despite three generations that surrounded him, Frost did not seem to visitors ancient or patriarchal. They said that he wore his years lightly and that his humor ran strong and young.

In his late 80's Frost was still strong and solid. Time had marked his face but it still showed strength and sensitivity, crowned with white, luxuriant hair. Deafness afflicted him but the blue eyes were still keen. He was a delight to photographers in his Ripton costume of blue slacks, gray sweater, and white shirt open at the throat.

Frost followed no routine in the months he spent in Vermont. All his life he has been a late sitter-up at night, a late-riser in the morning. He kept no hours during the day and did not even have a desk to work at. He was pretty free of letter-writing, too. Occasionally he dictated a letter but that was the extent of his correspondence. He never learned to use a typewriter and he did not like tape recorders. When he wrote poetry, he did it the old way with a pen, the way Emerson and Wordsworth wrote their poems in first draft.

His conversation at Ripton ranged widely, as it always had. A writer sent from the *Saturday Evening Post* who visited him in 1960 found him ready to talk on Castro and the high jumper, John Thomas; on farming and the beatniks; on the Boston Red Sox and Russia; on loneliness, religion and love— and these were only a broad sampling of the many topics they touched on, from the profound to the simple.

In the fall Frost struck out on a "lecture" tour, sometimes going as far as California, visiting 20 to 25 places on the way. He never lectured; he has never written out a lecture. He talked and he "said" his poems. The talks were carefully prepared but always seemed impromptu.

Winter found him in South Miami where he owned two

modest houses and some pines and orange trees. Between the Florida and Vermont sojourns, he stayed in his Cambridge, Massachusetts, home.

In 1958 Frost was appointed Consultant in Poetry to the Library of Congress—a fitting post for one who had become America's most representative poet. When his one-year term was over, he was appointed for three years to a new post at the Library of Congress, that of Consultant in the Humanities. "It sets me up mightily," Frost said in accepting this post, "that my venture into the capital of my country wasn't for nothing."

Frost's most notable act in his term as Consultant in Poetry at the Library of Congress was his intervention with the government to set free his old friend, Ezra Pound. Pound, who had befriended Frost and so many others when they were first knocking on the door of fame, was desperately in need of powerful friends. An exile in Italy for many years, Pound had broadcast talks from Rome during World War II that were regarded as treasonable by our government. He was indicted for treason, arrested in Italy, and brought back to the United States for trial after the war ended. But he was never tried for treason. Instead he was taken to court to determine if he was of unsound mind—psychiatrists who examined him found him mildly insane—and a jury returned the verdict: "Unsound mind." That had been in 1946.

For 12 years afterwards Pound was virtually a prisoner in St. Elizabeth's Hospital in Washington, D.C. He had to be presumed innocent of treason until proved guily in a trial; yet he could never be brought to trial so long as he was of unsound mind. His friends tried to get him released from St. Elizabeth's but Frost seems to have had the most weight. He called on Attorney General William P. Rogers.

"I'm here to get Ezra Pound out," he said.

Afterwards he told a friend: "They saw I was going to sit there until they did something about it—and they did."

On April 14, 1958, a motion was filed in the United States District Court for the District of Columbia for dismissal of the 13-year-old indictment of Pound. It was supported by a statement by Frost, with which a number of prominent writers and poets associated themselves. A few days later the indictment was dismissed and Pound was free to return to Europe to live out his old age.

A short time after Frost had recited in bold, strong tones "The Gift Outright" at President Kennedy's Inauguration, he was flown to Israel for a 10-day visit—not to see sights, he insisted, but to gain insights. He went there to serve as the first Samuel Paley Lecturer in American Culture and Civilization at the Hebrew University of Jerusalem. But he announced at once to a surprised audience of Israeli intellectuals that he would not talk about American civilization. "I *am* American civilization," he said, and it did not sound egotistic, because Frost is so obviously a symbol of his native land.

The Israeli newspapers called his visit a great success. He met the President of Israel and talked about farming. He held an informal seminar with university students. He explained that all his poems started with an idea. "An idea—now ask me what that is." He didn't wait. "An idea is a thought-felt thing." He liked that. "Never said it before," he said half to himself, half to his audience. Then he told them what a poem must contain. "Self-surprise," he called it. His two "lectures" at the Hebrew University were sell-outs.

In the university's guest book he wrote: "Something there is that does not love a wall—it is friendship. With eternal friendship. Robert Frost."

For months plans were made for the eighty-eighth birthday of Robert Frost. If January 20, 1961, had been a day of days for his cause of poetry, then, his friends decided, March 26, 1962 should be a day of days for Frost the man. On that day appeared his eleventh book of poetry, *In the Clearing,* in a huge printing of 50,000 copies. And on the morning of that day the ageless poet met the press at the Library of Congress where an exhibition of his life and works was opening. From the Library of Congress he was taken to the White House, bearing with him an inscribed copy of *In the Clearing* to give to President Kennedy. But the President had a birthday gift for the Grand Old Man of Poetry. It was the Congressional Medal voted by Congress in recognition of Frost's contribution to American letters.

"I suppose," the President said with a twinkle, "that you are disappointed that it was not a more controversial decision, but a unanimous one. It was the only thing they've been able to agree on for a long time."

"This is a great, great, great thing," said the poet as he took the medal from its case.

In the evening of this day of days, more than two hundred leaders of government and the world of letters honored Frost at a dinner, given by Secretary of the Interior Udall and Mrs. Udall and the publishing house of Holt, Rinehart and Winston. They drank a toast proposed by Chief Justice Earl Warren to Robert Frost, "the All American and all time poet."

Adlai E. Stevenson, U. S. Ambassador to the United Na-

[*189*]

tions, made a speech of tribute. "In Robert Frost, I daresay the American people have found their poet, their seer, their singer—in short, their bard."

For the moment, that is the last word on the life of this great man. But the poet promises in the last poem of *In the Clearing* that he means to strike many a blow yet—"why, I have four books coming. Don't worry about me," he said after the dinner.

In winter in the woods alone
Against the trees I go.
I mark a maple for my own
And lay the maple low.

At four o'clock I shoulder axe
And in the afterglow
I link a line of shadowy tracks
Across the tinted snow.

I see for Nature no defeat
In one tree's overthrow
Or for myself in my retreat
For yet another blow.